# Breaking and Training Young Horses

This book is to be returned on or before
the last date stamped below.

# BREAKING & TRAINING YOUNG HORSES

## CHRISTOPHER & VICTORIA COLDREY

The Crowood Press

First published in 1990 by
The Crowood Press Ltd
Ramsbury, Marlborough
Wiltshire SN8 2HR

This impression 1994

British Library Cataloguing-in-Publication Data

Coldrey, Christopher
  Breaking and training young horses.
  1. Livestock: Horses, Training
  I. Title II. Coldrey, Victoria
  636.1083

  ISBN 1 85223 286 2

Line-drawings by Matthew Lawrence

Typeset by Alacrity Phototypesetters, Banwell Castle,
Weston-super-Mare, Avon
Printed in Great Britain by Redwood Books,
Trowbridge, Wiltshire

# Contents

Acknowledgements     6
Foreword     7
Introduction     11

**Part 1   The Universal Start**

1 Before Starting     17
2 Preparation     28
3 Lungeing     36
4 Rollering     44
5 Long Reins     61
6 Backing and Riding Away     80
7 The Follow-Up and Cantering     93

**Part 2   Further Progress**

8 Keeping Your Young Horse Well     103
9 The First Branch of the Tree — Racing     111
10 Next Stages     118
11 Conversion of Ex-Racehorses     122
12 Conclusion     127

Appendix 1     132
Appendix 2     136

Index     143

# Acknowledgements

Our grateful thanks are due to all our staff at Herringswell Blood-stock Centre who so patiently and enthusiastically co-operated in producing the horses for the photographs in this book. We all had great fun doing this and the fact that they were taken over just a day and a half is a great credit to them as it is, too, to Anthony Reynolds LBIPP, LMPA. All the pictures are his and they support the text to perfection. We are grateful too, to Mark Rose AWCF and his assistant Daren Rose Dip. WCF for their help with the piece about horses' feet. Also to Carol Whitwood MCSP for allowing us to photograph her at work. Above all, our gratitude goes to all the owners and trainers who have trusted us with their lovely horses.

# Foreword

## BY SIR MARK PRESCOTT, BT.

It was my very good fortune, as a fourteen-year-old, to start my career in racing with the late Syd Kernick in Devon. A struggling National Hunt trainer, he supplemented a meagre income from racing by specialising in breaking-in difficult horses who came to his Kingsteignton yard from all over the country. A master of horse psychology, with a gift for an inventive approach, he was something of a genius in his sphere.

In more recent times, horsemen all over Britain were impressed by the method of 'starting' horses demonstrated by the American, Monty Roberts, whose countrywide displays showed a previously untouched horse, supplied locally, ridden away in less than an hour.

Both of these men used their extraordinary gifts, supplemented by years of experience, to cope with their own special circumstances. In Syd Kernick's case, he was taking over an animal on whom conventional methods had failed. As no matador should be expected to face a bull who has been fought before, so no horseman relishes the task of taking on a horse who commonplace procedures have failed to break-in. Often the horse had suffered at the hands of incompetents, sometimes he possessed an unusual degree of original sin, occasionally he suffered from a less than well-balanced brain. Frequently a combination of all three of these factors contributed to his journey to Kernick's South Devon yard.

The technique of Monty Roberts has been fashioned and perfected in the wide open spaces of the United States. There, any subsequent deviations by the equine pupil could be remedied, without excessive danger to man or beast, by a competent rough-rider, far from the rushing traffic and confined spaces of modern Britain.

For the ordinary mortal, it is probably prudent only to admire from afar such masters of their craft, whilst occasionally extracting an ingredient or two from their own individualistic method to incorporate into a more prosaic system.

There is, however, one vital thread common to every approach —
the appreciation of the fact that everything to do with horsemanship
is based upon a confidence trick. The smallest pony is twice as strong
as any man. He could drag a man anywhere at any time. He could
dislodge the most skilful horseman at will. When he has been properly broken-in, the only reason he does not do so is that he does not
believe that he can. From time immemorial, every successful method
of breaking-in horses to serve man's requirements has been founded
upon this deception which must be safeguarded and nurtured at
every stage. Upon this belief each stage of the process is built.
Mutual confidence follows and a partnership is formed.

Those responsible for the early education of the horse bear a
heavy responsibility. Quite rightly, in these days of growing concern
for animal welfare, the ultimate fate of the horse is given increasing
importance. This applies particularly to animals found wanting on
the racecourse. It is a sobering fact that only one in seven of the
thoroughbred horses conceived with a racing career in mind, whatever their cost of production, will ever win a race. Most will
eventually have to seek a career in some other section of the equine
sphere.

Sadly, no practical, professional horseman can be responsible for
every horse who passes through his care from the date of his foaling
to his eventual demise. However, it is his duty, to both the horse and
his owner, to ensure that everything possible is done during the
period of his early education to produce a willing, confident, biddable
and forward-going animal.

Such horses win significantly more than do their cowardly, hard-
pulling and intractable counterparts. Further, as a good ride, however limited their inherent abilities may have been, their days will
almost invariably be ended in a caring home. The end for a poor ride
is parlous in the extreme. Mankind owes such a horse no less than
the best start possible.

In this invaluable book Christopher and Victoria Coldrey have set
out, with brevity and clarity, a standard method which will suit
almost every horse and which any competent amateur can follow.
Adhered to carefully, it will ensure that the horse commences his
career with a sound grounding, suited to whichever branch of the
equine world he may eventually be directed. The illustrations in this
book are superb and the text concise. There is much for the professional, indeed for us all, for as Picasso once said: 'Anyone who is
entirely self-taught had a poor teacher indeed.'

## Foreword

It is some eight years since I first sent my few yearlings to the Coldreys' establishment, five miles east of Newmarket, at Herrings-well. I was their first customer. Since then, aided by their family and a highly motivated staff, they have built up their business to be the largest breaking yard in the country. Their success has been founded on hard work, diligence and, above all, a sound method that has produced highly successful equine graduates in every field. They are now patronised by the largest and most powerful training stables in the land and break-in over a hundred horses a year. As ever, results have yielded their reward. Few, if any, are better qualified to write a book such as this.

*M.P.*
*Heath House*
*Newmarket*
*Suffolk*

Fig 1  Christopher and Victoria Coldrey with their homebred
Advanced Event horse, Polly's Folly.

# Introduction

If you listen to champion racehorse trainer Henry Cecil, you will hear the same message coming through again and again – the key to success is having happy horses and happy horses live in cheerful yards with smiling staff. 'Your prayer must be that you may have a sound mind in a sound body. Pray for a bold spirit . . .', wrote Juvenal almost two thousand years ago. This is exactly what we want to achieve in the training of our horses. Everyone knows that you cannot produce your best if you feel below par. So, with the horse, the first priority is that he must feel physically well. He must find life and learning easy and he must find it enjoyable. Achieve this and you are half-way to having a good horse on your hands.

The purpose of this book is to outline what we believe is the best way of 'starting' horses from their earliest days, through breaking and riding away, to the time they are ready to go on to whatever is the next specialist stage of their career. We believe that the system is right for all horses; that they should all be started the same whether they are going to be racehorses, polo ponies, show-jumpers or dressage specialists.

Before we go any deeper it is necessary to agree about terminology. The word *breaking* is an emotive one and does not mean what it says. In non-horsy circles it is one that we do not much like to use. It is slightly softened when referred to as *breaking-in* but this does not sound very professional. Monty Roberts, the talented American horseman who recently toured Britain and claimed to have backed 5,400 horses uses *starting*, a word we much prefer and the one which we shall use instead of breaking for the rest of this book.

As virtually all the work we do at Herringswell is with racehorses, the word *training* here refers to the process of preparing horses for racing and is not to be confused with *schooling* which is the physical process of teaching a horse to do specific things. *Dressage* is a French word meaning schooling, but here will refer to the formal art of refining the horse's natural paces for exhibition or competition. The word *man* means *Homo sapiens* and includes both sexes! When talking about a horse, the word 'he' is used in preference to 'it', which is too impersonal and in this case, too, refers to either sex.

Many people in Britain have seen the demonstrations by Monty Roberts in which he takes an unbroken (unstarted) youngster and has it ridden away in 35 minutes. It is a really exciting display by a very gifted horseman. We take two to three weeks to do all that he does in that short time. As you will read, it is all done with the greatest care and attention to detail. At the end, we believe that by this classical method, all good horsemen can make almost any horse a happy, confident and correct ride who will be able to go on to the next stage in his development. Nothing is gained by backing the horse straight away when he is neither physically nor mentally ready to be ridden, especially if it is done by someone without the American's very special gifts.

The art of riding is like a tree. The tap root is the centuries-old affinity between man and horse. The smaller roots are what an individual may bring to his pursuit of perfection in the study of this extraordinary animal that so obsesses us. Fed by these roots we come to the base of the trunk which is where all horses must start. All ascend the trunk until they are started, backed and ridden away. In the case of flat racehorses, this is done while they are still yearlings or two-year-olds. In the case of other horses, the age at which they should be started is a matter for debate and is discussed in detail in Chapter 1.

It is the flat horses, then, who first branch off but before they do so they must, in common with all others, be able to go forward, go straight and go calmly on their own and in company at walk, trot and canter. The trunk of our tree is the classical method of schooling which has been handed down for successive generations, starting long before the birth of Christ, wonderfully described by the Greek horsemaster and author Xenophon and culminating in the Grand Prix dressage horse of today. At different stages of this classical line, horses branch off for the specialist training required for whatever discipline or sport is to be their *métier*.

So, although this book is largely about the starting of young racehorses, the system, method and principles apply exactly to any horse of any age.

We have divided the book into two parts. The first, called 'The Universal Start', applies to all horses whatever their ultimate use is going to be. The second, 'Further Progress' goes on to discuss

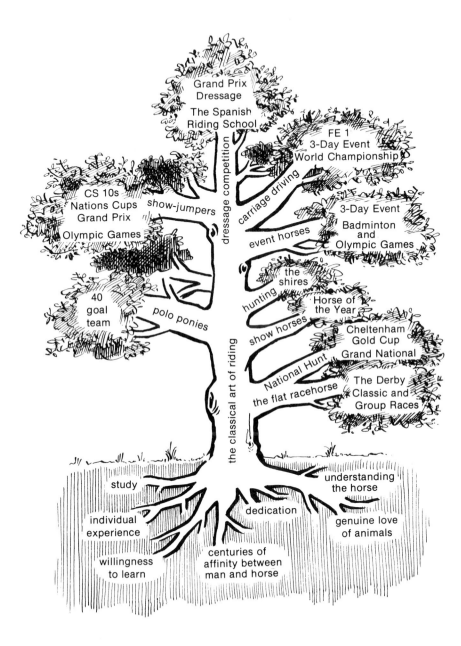

Fig 2  The tree of classical riding.

specific work for the special uses to which the horses are to be put. We follow them a part of the way along the branch as they come off the main trunk of our tree. We stop only a short way along the branch, for that is where a specialist can happily take over with a horse who has had 'a fair start'.

# PART 1

# THE UNIVERSAL START

# 1
# Before Starting

Before we get into the intricacies of starting it is fascinating to read what Xenophon wrote about preparing horses for the 'horse-breaker'. We found this piece after we had written this first chapter and we were amazed to see how little has changed and how similar are the minimum requirements for a horse sent in to be broken today to what they were twenty-three centuries ago.

It does not seem necessary for me to describe the method of breaking a colt, because those who are enlisted in the cavalry in our states are persons of very considerable means, and take no small part in the government. It is also a great deal better than being a horse-breaker for a young man to see that his own condition and that of his horse is good, or if he knows this already, to keep up his practice in riding; while an old man had better attend to his family and friends, to public business and military matters, than be spending his time in horse-breaking. The man, then, that feels as I do about horse-breaking will, of course, put out his colt. He should not put him out, however, without having a written contract made, stating what the horse is to be taught before he is returned, just as he does when he puts his son out to learn a trade. This will serve as a reminder to the horse-breaker of what he must attend to, if he is to get his fee.

See to it that the colt be kind, used to the hand, and fond of men when he is put out to the horse-breaker. He is generally made so at home and by the groom, if the man knows how to manage, so that solitude means to the colt hunger and thirst and teasing horseflies, while food, drink and relief from pain come from man. For if this be done, colts must not only love men, but even long for them. Then, too, the horse should be stroked in the places which he most likes to have handled; that is, where the hair is thickest, and where he is least able to help himself if anything hurts him. The groom should also be directed to

17

Fig 3   Xenophon.

lead him through crowds, and to make him familiar with
all sorts of sights and all sorts of noises. Whenever the colt
is frightened at any of them, he should be taught, not by
irritating but by soothing him, that there is nothing to
fear. It seems to me that this is enough to tell the amateur
to do in the matter of horse-breaking.
> Xenophon, *The Art of Horsemanship* translated by
> M. H. Morgan Ph.D. (J. A. Allen, 1979)

At Herringswell we get around a hundred yearlings and two-
year-olds to start each year, and what a variety they are. It soon
becomes obvious that, although breeding plays a large part, the
temperament of the horse is hugely affected by the treatment he
has received before he arrives with us.

The first to come in are the American yearlings who have been

18

Fig 4   American yearlings — very little surprises or outrages
them and the starting process is usually very smooth.

bought in July and August to be trained in Britain. Generally, these
are the easiest, for not only do they seem to have been well handled,
but by the time they reach us they have had so much happen to them
– travelling, flying, strange stables, strange humans, being inspected, vetted, sold, examined – that very little surprises or outrages
them and the starting process is usually very smooth.

   Much the same applies to yearlings from the Highflyer and October Sales in Newmarket. Many of these have been professionally prepared, are in excellent physical shape and are easy to start
and ride away. The result is a happy one for both owners and
trainers who are going to take over later on. We all like youngsters to
show a bit of spirit and the courage that is a vital ingredient in the
make-up of a good racehorse, but this is quite a different thing from
the one who fights back because life has become full of fearful
change. There is no doubt that the more foals and yearlings become
accustomed to people, to being handled, led about and gently but
firmly disciplined so that they both trust and respect their handlers,
the better the starting process is going to be – and probably the

better the end result. We have received horses for starting who have taken up to 30 minutes to get off the horse-box and into a stable. They are literally paralysed with fear. Just as a child is prepared at playschool or kindergarten for more serious education, so a young horse should be made ready for going away to be started and trained from the very beginning of its life.

## MINIMUM REQUIREMENTS

The very minimum that a youngster should learn before being started is:

**Leading**   To be led first with his mother and, after weaning, on his own, so that he will go where the handler wants without resisting.

Fig 5   1988 chestnut colt, by Diesis, ex Informatique, owned
by Sir Gordon White and to be trained by Henry Cecil,
shows what is to be expected of a yearling before coming in
for starting. Here, he is being led up.

**Standing**  To stand still and correctly while being looked at by people. To walk and trot in hand.

**Tie up**  To stand in the box tied up to a piece of string by his lead rope. We never use chains as they are the cause of many injuries and accidents.

**Feet**  To lift up his feet for picking out on demand and to accept trimming by the farrier.

**Grooming**  To accept and to enjoy the process of grooming.

**People**  To become accustomed to people (individually and in groups) and not to be worried by the things that go with them, like dogs, noise and vehicles.

All of this is not just to make life easier for whoever is doing the starting but, more importantly, in the interests of safety. Many of the yearlings we have received over the years have been downright dangerous. It is shameful for the staff at studs to be allowed to put both people and young horses at risk when they go in for starting because they cannot be bothered to teach them the rudiments of

Fig 6  Standing still and correctly.

Fig 7 Always tie horses to a piece of string and never straight on to the tie ring.

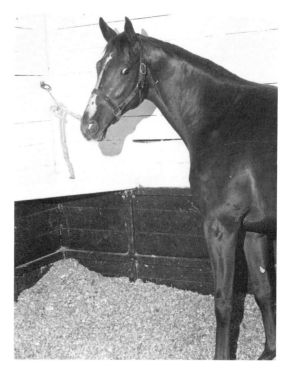

Fig 8 Trimming by the farrier, Mark Rose, AWCF who looks after the horses' feet at Herringswell.

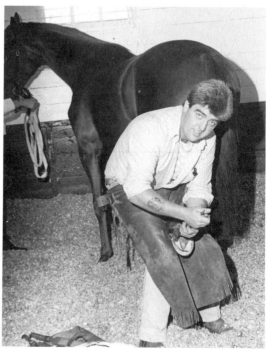

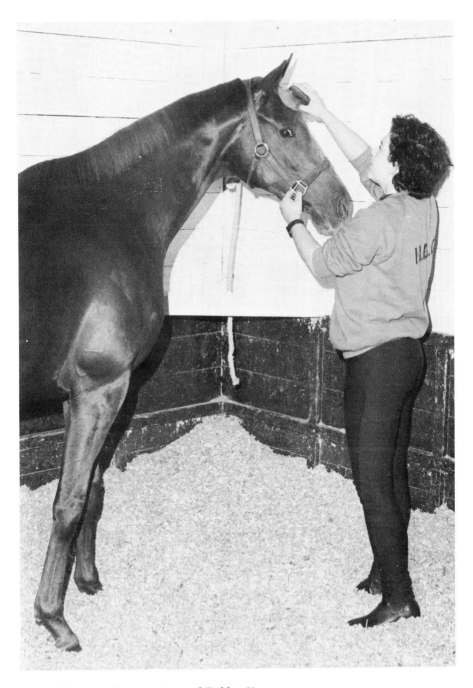

Fig 9   Enjoying the attentions of Debbie Kay.

Fig 10   This yearling, having travelled from the USA, was
used to people, dogs, etc.

good manners. Thoroughbred yearlings have, with justice, been
described as four-legged accidents waiting to happen. Anything
which helps to avoid these accidents can only be highly desirable.

Breeders looking for characteristics that make a good racehorse on
the track pay scant attention to temperament. There is not a shadow
of doubt that certain horses – both stallions and mares – produce
offspring who are really difficult to start. The problem that they
present is compounded if the animal concerned is not handled
enough or properly beforehand. In some cases, it is difficult to do all
this where a horse is born and bred, but owners would be right, we
believe, to insist on minimum requirements being met – especially
with a youngster whose breeding makes it likely that he will be a
difficult customer. Where these standards cannot be met and a
yearling is destined to be sold at auction, it is well worth considering
having him professionally prepared. Unfortunately, though, costs
are high and unless a good price is justifiably expected it is unlikely to
be a viable proposition.

Fig 11   Bottle-fed foals are often difficult later on.

---

**Watch Point**

Bottle-fed foals are often difficult later on. They have been spoilt at a very early age because the handler feels sorry for them. They can, thus, turn into bullies, especially colts, and always expect to get their own way. A four-year-old hunter we were asked to start was a prime example of this, to the point that he refused to go into his stable on arrival. He was big, strong, pushy and definitely prepared to argue about anything he did not approve of. He was typically a horse brought up on a bottle by a weak woman! But we eventually came to mutual agreement that his job was to be ridden, and he went on to carry his owner hunting really well.

---

On the subject of sending a horse to be started by a professional, we find it incomprehensible that studs and owners send yearlings of the greatest value with no sort of protective gear whatsoever. The result is animals arriving with scrapes and gashes where they have injured themselves loading or unloading. This often delays the starting process for a week or more, even if there is no serious injury. What a complete waste of time and money.

Readers will have noted that lungeing has not been listed among the minimum requirements. A horse being prepared for sale by auction should be taught to lunge, if only as a preparation for the wind test. For this, the unfortunate animal is chased around the lunge ring to see if his breathing is normal. One sees some horrific exhibitions when this is done, but the horror is alleviated if the yearling concerned has been taught to lunge correctly. By and large, though, we prefer to receive horses who have not been lunged, for two reasons. Firstly, you do not want them to be too fit to start with so that, in the event of a battle of wills, they will submit more readily. Secondly because the serious business of starting begins with lungeing and it is here that the starter first forges a relationship with the horse.

## AT WHAT AGE TO START?

Flat racehorses, who are going to run as two-year-olds if all goes well, are started either as yearlings between September and the end of the year or in the first two or three months of their two-year-old life. Later foals or backward yearlings lose nothing by delaying their start until the New Year.

Coming from a background of disciplines other than flat racing, we always thought that the starting of such very young animals was unfortunate but inevitable because they must start their career at two. However, after several years of experience we are firmly of the opinion that if we bought a foal even to be a Grand Prix dressage horse we would still start him as a two-year-old and, having ridden him away and cantered with a seven-stone lad or lass, turn him away for another year before bringing him back to carry on again.

The reasons for this should be clear from what has already been said in this chapter. A two-year-old who has been well started is so much more biddable, is more mature, has an improved physique and carriage, fears nothing and above all will never forget the simple lessons learned which will stand him in good stead for the rest of his life.

Starting older horses can be a much harder task because they are bigger and stronger and, not having had any discipline are often very hard work indeed. We recently started a six-year-old pony who had stood in a field with a friend for four years. She was a really piggy, awkward one to do and clearly should have been started years earlier. The worst of the problem was the separation from her friend. This required a weaning process more prolonged than separating a foal from his dam because they had been together for such a long time.

# 2

# Preparation

When a horse arrives for starting, we know very little about him and owners do not always tell you the truth. In addition, the change of environment may well upset the new arrival for the first twenty-four hours or so. For this reason we never take the headcollar off an unstarted newcomer. If, inadvertently, it is removed from a really nervous young horse, it can be the very devil of a job to catch the horse and put it back on – and you will have opened your relationship with a battle. This is a very bad thing because the art of starting,

Fig 12   It can be the devil of a job to catch the horse and put the headcollar back on.

indeed the art of schooling all horses, is to avoid a battle through the use of our superior brainpower. Horses are stronger and quicker than humans, but we can think faster, so we ought to know what a horse might do before he has thought of it. Horses are, above all things, creatures of habit and going well and behaving well is a habit. Behaving badly is a bad habit and one that is difficult to turn around. We should, therefore, always think ahead so that the horse is not put in a situation which he is likely to resent. We should make it easy for the horse to understand what is wanted and to obey. At every stage, the less resistance you have, the better you are doing your job. The horse must be fooled into doing what you want because it is easy, because he knows what is being asked and because he has become accustomed to obeying without any fuss.

As we shall see, there are phases in the starting process which virtually all horses resent and fight against. In particular, the first time they feel the roller (surcingle) round them they all go off in a series of huge bucks, often roaring like a lion as they go. It is a marvellous and fearful spectacle but does not generally last for more than a few circuits of the lunge ring.

## THE FIRST FEW DAYS

First make him feel settled and comfortable in mind and body. A good deep, clean bed, plenty of clean water, first-class hay ad-lib and a cheerful but not too noisy environment are the order of the day. If horses have had a long journey, especially a long flight, we always give them electrolytes in their evening feed for a few days.

---

**Watch Point**

Electrolytes replace the salts lost from the body as a result of stress. In particular, they prevent a horse becoming dehydrated or help to recover from dehydration. We feed electrolytes: twice a week all year round; every day in very hot weather; any day when a horse has sweated freely; before, during and after long journeys. The event horses are dosed every day during competition. We always put the electrolytes in the feed and not in the water because this way you know the dose has been taken. Half-used buckets of water are thrown out and with it goes the expensive electrolytes.

---

29

Fig 13   If you were suddenly to give a group of
just-ridden-away horses an extra scoop of oats in the
evening feed, you could confidently expect the highest of
high jinks the next morning.

We do not feed hard food to horses who are just being started. This is
to avoid trouble and encourage good behaviour. We do not want
them too fit and we do not want them to be above themselves. That
is a certain way of inviting accidents. One of the extraordinary
things about very young horses is the very rapid reaction to
increases in hard food intake (oats, cubes etc.) So we slowly introduce these feeds into the horses' diet over the whole starting period,
only very gradually increasing the quantity as they show us that
they are ready for more. If you were suddenly to give a group of just-
ridden-away yearlings an extra scoop of oats in their evening feed
you could confidently expect the highest of high jinks the next
morning.

If a yearling has had a long journey we will probably leave him in
the box for the first day or perhaps lead him out for a pick of nice
grass. Those who have flown in from the USA, for example, are
always jet lagged and will usually lie down all that first day. This is a

good chance for whoever is looking after the horse to get to know him and to make friends. A good lad or lass can get things away to a fine start by doing everything right on this important day.

---

### Watch Point

Yearlings or horses who are travelling long distances can get colic, caused by stress during travelling. A dose of liquid paraffin before travelling is very beneficial.

Never let anybody, especially girls, get too familiar with colts. They **must** learn to respect people and to stand away from them when they come into the box. Girls should not wear perfume while on duty with colts as this excites them and they become difficult and randy. Fillies can be petted as much as you like – it only does them good – but definitely not colts.

---

## Teeth

You need to have your horse settled before you can ask your vet to inspect and rasp his teeth. In yearlings, rasping will always be necessary. The sooner you can get it done, the more comfortable he will be in his mouth. We get all of ours done at the earliest possible stage in the starting process as we feel that, if possible, you should not put a bit in a horse's mouth until the razor sharp edges on his molars have been rasped away. You cannot expect a calm head carriage from a horse with a mouth that hurts.

As soon as the horse has recovered from the journey, work can begin. The first lesson is lungeing.

## THE LUNGE RING

The lunge ring must be quite large. Ours are all around fifty to sixty feet (16 – 20m) in diameter. Working on small circles puts a horse under great strain, especially on the hock-joint, and lungeing in a small ring is a good recipe for producing thoroughpins. All of our lunge rings have high wooden walls which help the horse to keep his balance and encourage him to concentrate on what he is doing and not on what is going on outside. The going must not be too hard nor, indeed, too deep. Heavy going in the lunge ring puts a completely unacceptable strain on the horse's limbs and joints. Regular harrowing is a must to keep the going level.

## TACKING UP

Never try tacking up on your own to start with. Always have two people until the process has been completely accepted. The first thing required is a really good lungeing cavesson. Do not try to lunge off a headcollar or bridle. All of our cavessons have a mouthing bit and we always lunge off two reins. The top rein goes on to the ring on top of the noseband and the bottom rein on to the ring of the connecting link that joins the rings of the bit. The cavesson is fitted carefully over the headcollar. This may seem an awful lot of tackle on

Fig 14  The cavesson fitted over the headcollar. Note the browband and two lunge reins.

the horse's head, but is very necessary. The youngster will probably be a bit suspicious of what you are doing and if, having taken off the headcollar, you lose him before you have got the cavesson on, you are in trouble straightaway. So leave the headcollar on until you are sure that the cavesson will be accepted without fuss or demur. The cavesson must eventually have a browband. If your horse is in the least bit head-shy it is better to leave the browband off for the first few days. Again, this avoids a battle until you can slip it on without problems.

---

### Watch Point

If he is really difficult, leave a browband on his headcollar. To do this without losing the yearling put another headcollar with a browband on top of the first one of the horse's head and slide the original one off afterwards. This enables you to keep hold of a difficult customer throughout the change-over.

---

So, you have the cavesson with two reins ready. We have a rule for all horses that whenever they are lunged, if they are shod, they must wear brushing boots – behind as well as in front. At this stage your young horse will be unshod. Nevertheless, a pair of boots should be put on in front. Now the feet are picked out, the mane and tail brushed out and we are ready to go for the first lesson. We make it a rule to pick out the feet both before and after each day's exercise. They will also be done when the horse is dressed over. So, at least three times a day he will be made to pick up his feet for us and after a few days it will have become second nature. To avoid burning your hands you should wear gloves when lungeing or long reining. Never use nylon headcollars, lead reins or lunge reins. If the horse pulls away it can result in serious burns.

Take up the two lunge reins and loop them together as if they were one. Hold the bunch of reins in your left hand and lead the horse with your right hand. He must learn to go in and out of the box quietly, carefully and straight so that he does not bang his hip in the doorway. If he hurts himself once going in and out you can give yourself long-term problems, so take special care. Incidentally, stable doors should be a minimum of 4ft (1.3m) wide. Now you have reached the lunge ring, you have shut the gate and are ready to start work.

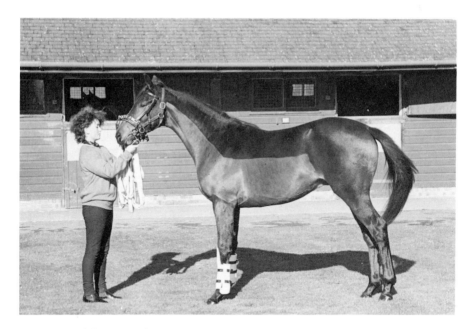

Fig 15   Trifolio (1987) bay colt by Touching Wood, ex
Triple Reef; owned by Mr Jose M. Soriano, trained by
Henry Cecil and prepared for lungeing by Marion Davey
(an ex-pupil of the British Racing School).

---

**Watch Point**

Never take short cuts. This is how accidents occur. If you need
help with anything you are doing with a horse, get it. Do not
battle on by yourself until something goes wrong. It is not
brave, only stupid.

---

## PRAISE AND THE USE OF THE VOICE

Horses are very responsive to the human voice – not just the words,
but especially the tone. Try to use the same words all the time when
you are starting. Just like people, the great spur to get horses to try
to do their best is praise. Be lavish with it and accompany the praising
voice with strokes and pats so that they know they have done well
and that you are pleased with them. They bask in praise and will
eventually do everything they can to earn it from you.

# TITBITS

We never give young colts titbits (sugar, apples, Polo mints) because, unfortunately, it often results in people getting bitten. Later on in life and for fillies or geldings it is fine, but it is natural for a colt to bite – he does it to the object of his love, doesn't he? – and he has to be trained not to do it. It is not part of training to give him sweets.

# 3

# Lungeing

The reason that we use two reins for lungeing are threefold. Firstly, because it is safer. If one rein breaks or the buckle breaks or comes undone you still have the other available to you. (This is not as far fetched as you might think when you see what some of them get up to.) Secondly, the rein which is attached indirectly to the rings of the bit is a good brake should you need it. The horse is worked from the rein on the noseband, with the bit rein kept slack unless required. Thirdly, the horse becomes used to two reins so when you go on to driving in the reins the transition is not so dramatic (for the horse!). Using a single rein from one bit ring over the top of the head to the other bit ring results in a young green mouth being ruined before you have even backed the animal. If he pulls away or runs off, the bit tightens in the mouth and causes pain for all the wrong reasons. It is much easier to discipline a young horse with the top rein of the cavesson without touching his mouth. A good sharp tug on that rein is very effective and does not hurt at all.

## HOLDING THE REINS

You must practise this a great deal before attempting to lunge or long rein. To lead a horse, hold both reins in your right hand below the bit and drop the rest on the ground. Then loop the reins into your right hand. When all the rein is in your right hand transfer the looped reins into your left hand and lead the horse with your right hand.

This is very complicated to read but it must become second nature, otherwise you can get your hands or fingers badly damaged if they get caught up. The object is for the rein to come out of your hand in the right way. Reverse this to lunge on the right rein but use the first way to lunge to the left.

## LEFT-HANDED

The first thing to do once you have sorted out the reins is to lead the horse a couple of times around the ring on a left-handed circle. If you have a particularly difficult animal you are well advised to have one person leading and one with the reins. Virtually all horses go better and more easily to the left than to the right. Some trainers of horses think that the answer to this is to work them more on their bad rein and less on their good rein. In fact, the opposite is correct, just as it is wrong to force left-handed children to write with their right hand. The horse goes badly to the right because it is difficult and painful.

---

### Watch Point

Always practise with the reins attached to a lively human or easy-to-lunge old horse before trying yearlings with double reins. It is quite an art not to get tangled up. **Never** lunge with the rein held behind your back as you will quite likely put the horse's poll out with the leverage and cause unnecessary resistances through lack of direct and sensitive contact with the horse. A great deal of damage is done (unwittingly) by pulling horses' heads around too much and also, incidentally, if they run back when tied up. The physiotherapist will be very busy. (*See* Chapter 8.)

---

So, the correct treatment is to work the horse very little on the difficult rein, gradually increasing over quite a long period until the horse is equally happy in either direction. It is very important indeed to get this right. All horses must become ambidextrous so as to be able to cope with racecourses that, in Great Britain, are both left- and right-handed. For this reason, all of our horses are worked on both reins. We normally canter ridden horses twice – once to the left and once to the right — on our oval all-weather track.

## LUNGEING

Once you have led the horse around the ring a couple of times (with or without the helper, depending on the horse) you can start to lunge him to the left. You lead with the reins in your left hand and the lunge whip in your right hand. Never lead from the hand opposite to the direction in which you are lungeing. If you do, your body will be in the wrong position and facing the wrong direction relative to the horse. It is also certain that you will not be prepared for an emergency should it occur. The tension on the bit rein must be slacker than the one to the noseband at all times. You only use the bit rein to stop or slow down the horse if he is being inattentive or silly or bolting!

The art of lungeing lies mostly in the position of your body. When riding, you will have been taught to keep the horse between your legs and your hands. When lungeing, your leading hand (left hand when going to the left) corresponds to the rider's hands, and your right hand and whip, to the rider's legs. Thus, you should make an equal-sided triangle between your two hands and the nose and tail of the horse.

You will not, at first, be able to keep the horse out along the wall of the lunge ring if you stand in the middle. You must therefore walk

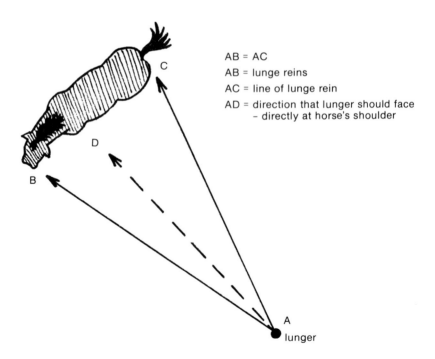

AB = AC
AB = lunge reins
AC = line of lunge rein
AD = direction that lunger should face
– directly at horse's shoulder

Fig 16  Ideal position of horse and lunger.

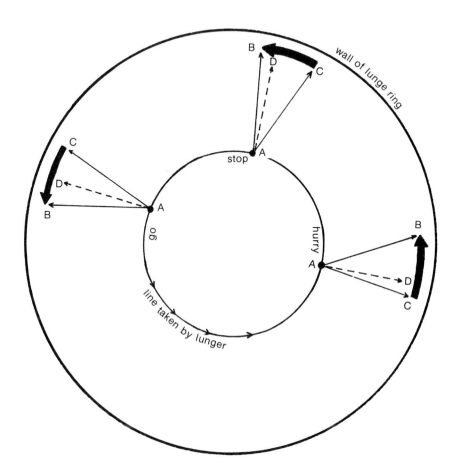

Fig 17 The lunger's position is very important since it affects the horse's momentum.

around on a smaller circle, maintaining your position as shown in Fig 18 so as to keep the horse moving steadily forward. If you get in front of the movement of the horse he will stop and if you get behind the movement he will speed up. The position of your body and where you are looking are extremely important. You will find that the easiest pace for the horse is the trot. Although he must walk in both directions from the very beginning of his training, on this first day he will probably only want to walk at the end of the session. After a day or two you will be able to walk him away from you at the outset.

Fig 18 Tropic Power (1987) bay colt, by Petorius, ex Investiture, owned by Mrs P.L. Young and trained by Bill O'Gorman. Note the boots all round and the large diameter of the ring which places much less strain on the horse's limbs.

In any case, on your first session let him trot and try to establish a rhythm as early as you possibly can. A total of about ten minutes is going to be sufficient on day 1. Unless he is particularly co-operative you will have done well enough if you walk and trot to the left, keeping your horse well out by the boards of the lunge ring.

---

### Watch Point

To keep the horse out on the circle step towards him and in the direction he is travelling, and at the same time drive him out to the boards. **Do not** step back as he makes the circle smaller; he will try to make a habit of running you over and damage his joints by working on too small a circle.

---

When your horse is going nicely in the lunge ring try to keep him going using a light hand. He will use the boards for balance and should learn to carry himself lightly and easily on a steady and gentle contact. The horse must not lean on the rein or use it to help keep balanced.

The sooner you can get the horse going well on the lunge, the sooner you can get to the next stage – rollering. That is putting on the roller or surcingle. You want to do this early on and before the horse is too fit. The quicker he accepts the roller, the less the likelihood of an accident. Aim for three days lungeing and roller on day 3 or 4, depending on progress. Before rollering, your horse should:

1.  Lunge at walk and trot on both reins.
2.  Stand, walk and trot on command.
3.  Change rein without undue fuss.

As with everything else, all this is achieved by the use of the aids. That is voice, hands, body position and the artificial aids — reins and lunge whip. Some people think that you should only lunge to the left until after the horse has been rollered. This is because you do not want to do anything that might encourage him to catch you unawares by spinning round and going off in the opposite direction during the process of rollering.

---

### Watch Point

**Always** make the horse halt out on the circle, especially colts. Many people make horses halt by pulling them into the centre or jerking violently on the reins and making the horse stop and turn in from the trot. In effect, this is one of the first lessons in teaching a horse to 'stop and whip round'. Do not do it. It is like being a lounge lizard, except we call them 'lazy lunge lizards'. In other words, lazy stable lads find it the easiest way to stop the horse, instead of teaching him proper downward transitions — this is **not** lungeing. We spend a lot of time teaching yearlings, who arrive having been lunged elsewhere, not to do this. We also call the people who make this mistake the 'trot and stop merchants'.

---

# COMMANDS

It is essential that everyone at one establishment uses the same commands and uses them in the same way. The ones we use are 'Stand', 'Walk' and 'Trot' and it is the tone used that is the important thing. (Never put an imaginary question mark to your command. 'Walk?' will never get the correct result as the horse will certainly answer with a negative.) In a very short time the horse will understand those three words. While he is learning them, use the body positions shown in Fig 18 and the commands together. Lowering the whip, point on the ground, will help slow down; raising it above the horizontal will help speed up; pointing it to the centre of the horse's body will tell him to move out towards the wall. Much of it is feel and cannot be written down, but with these guide-lines you should be able to achieve good results.

# TURNING ROUND

To turn round from left rein to right rein, first you must get your horse to stand. Do not let him turn in and come towards you. The reason for this is that it is quite possible, especially in the case of an angry colt, that he will come at you and he must be taught to stand on the circle and show respect for the handler. If the colt comes at you the reins will get round his legs as you cannot gather them up quickly enough. So, you should go to the horse, coiling in the reins as you go. When you come up, praise him and let him know he has done well and pat him gently but firmly on the neck. Now lead him back to the centre, change your leading hand, transfer your whip into your left hand, never for a moment taking your eye off the horse, and make him walk off on the right rein. If he goes off too fast, never mind – he will soon settle down. What he must **not** do is stop and turn round, so you must concentrate like fury and be very alert so as to keep him going forward all the time. He will find it difficult to the right and will turn around the moment you lose concentration. Be content with just a few circles and then, using the same technique, change back onto the easy rein again.

Two or three day's practice at this and you will be ready to roller. At some point, your horse will undoubtedly have cantered in the ring, probably disunited, when charging off or when some outside influence has surprised him, but **never** canter a young unfit horse on

42

a small circle on purpose. It imposes far too great a strain on the limbs.

Do not be tempted to work your young horse for too long. A few minutes on each rein is enough. They are very soft at this stage and very easy to spoil. Fifteen to twenty minutes from start to finish is ample time. Patience, persistence, concentration, quick thinking, consistent commands and tact will all be required of you, in abundance, over this vital period in a young horse's life. The rewards, though, can be really thrilling when you see him happily ridden away.

# 4

# Rollering

This is one of the two most important days in the whole starting process. The other is, of course, the day when the horse is first ridden away. Do not be in a hurry today – it may take longer than you anticipate. It is a job for two people, so never try to do it on your own. Have the tack ready and waiting, the roller, breastplate and pad. Never use a surcingle as it is not designed for this job. A proper breaking roller with a breastplate must be used.

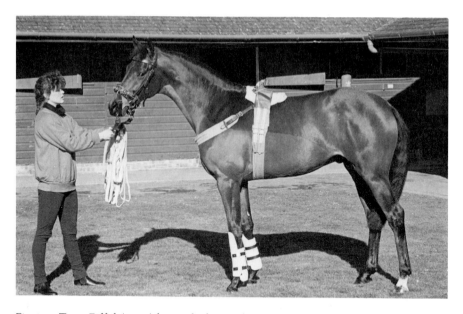

Fig 19   Tour Eiffel (1987) bay colt, by High Line, ex Gay France, owned by Sheikh Mohammed and trained by Henry Cecil. The roller is left on for three or four days so that the horse gets completely accustomed to the feel of it. Prepared by Mari-Lynn Bunker. Note that there is no head-collar under the cavesson as this horse was already ridden away at the time.

# THE FIRST STEPS

Bring your horse out and lunge him for a few minutes to settle him down. When he is going nicely get your helper in with the roller. You will start on the left rein. Whatever you do, do not be tentative but tackle the job as if you mean business – firmly but gently. Now the holder has both hands on the reins which are held pretty short so as to have control of the horse when he first feels the roller. Stand to the near side facing the side of the head and be prepared to hang on as you let out the reins. Do not get in front of your horse or you may find yourself flat on your back! Make sure the reins are coiled so that you can let them out easily and quickly.

Your helper now places the pad and the pad of the roller on the horse's back, immediately behind the withers. The roller should be moved around a bit so that the horse knows it is there and can already feel it. The girth of the roller is folded back on top of the pad and not left hanging down where it is likely to frighten him. Next, free the breast strap and reach under the neck with your left hand, bring it round and buckle it onto the front of the roller.

---

### Watch Point

Always avoid any situation in which a girth or surcingle can slip back around the horse's belly. If this happens it becomes a bucking strap or cinch and you have a very dangerous animal on your hands. This is the reason why the breastplate must be fastened before you attempt to do up the roller. It is also, incidentally, the reason why, when you take a rug off a horse you always start at the back and work forwards and when you put a rug on you start at the front and work backwards. Of course, your horse will not yet have been rugged up.

---

All the time you are doing this, talk to the horse. Let your tone of voice give him encouragement and confidence. Your helper should now let the roller down to hang on the right (opposite) side of the horse. Keeping out of harm's way, your helper should then reach under the horse and bring the roller through to the left side. While this is going on you want to hold the horse's attention and his confidence. The helper will gently but firmly buckle up the roller, loosely at first and then a hole at a time until it is done up, not tightly

45

Fig 20   Tropic Power again. This sequence shows Victoria and Charles Coldrey rollering. Here, the pad is placed (firmly) on the back just behind the withers.

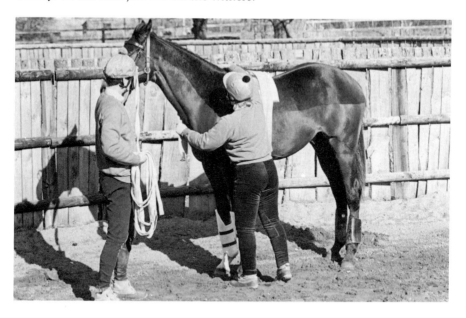

Fig 21   The girth is folded back so that it will not startle the horse by banging against his opposite side. Meanwhile, the breastplate is brought forward around the front of the horse.

Fig 22  The breastplate is buckled up to stop the roller from slipping back.

Fig 23  The girth is let down on the far (off) side. It must be let down gently but steadily so as not to alarm the horse.

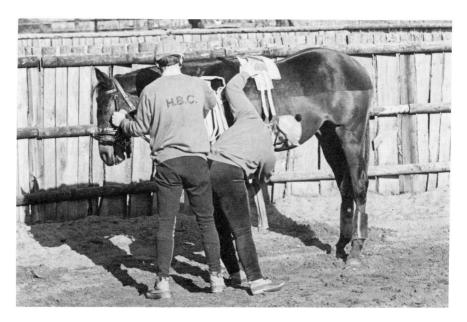

Fig 24   The girth is brought through underneath.

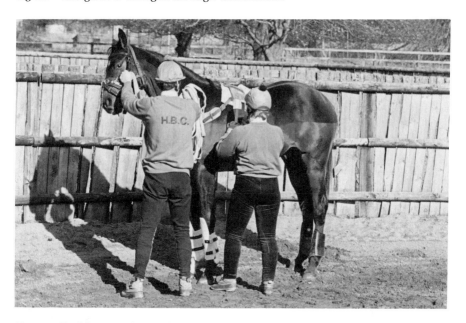

Fig 25   Buckling up the girth. Do not pull it up too tight at this stage but firmly enough not to slip when the horse moves off. Keep his head up so that he does not feel the roller until you are ready for him to go.

Fig 26   Now Victoria takes the whip in her right hand.

Fig 27   As the horse moves off, the helper is there with
the whip to make sure that he keeps going forward. Note
the positions and angles of the bodies of both people.

Fig 28   The lunger moves back and starts to lengthen the
reins while the helper continues to make sure that the
horse goes forward. Note the loose contact on the bit rein.
Both Charles and Victoria are positioned to keep him on
the boards and going forward. It is **not** normally necessary
to hit or touch the horse with the whip.

but tight enough to stay in position when the horse moves off. Now
your helper moves away a couple of feet and picks up the lunge whip
in the right hand. The horse will be very suspicious by now and as
you give him the order to walk on he will start to move, feel the roller
round his chest and POW! he will go off in a series of outraged bucks
to try to get rid of the new and infuriating restriction.

The two of you must work as a team to make sure that he does not
turn around or turn in and come at you. You have the reins, your
helper has the whip and, between you, you must keep him moving
forward around the outside of the lungeing circle. After a short time
he will settle down and pick up the rhythm of his trot again. Praise
him when he does this and let him know that he has done well. This
is the time when obedience really counts because it is much easier to
get him back into a rhythm by command as it is what he has been
taught. Do not be surprised if a colt roars; some fillies will squeal and
almost scream. One filly, who is now quite well known, sat down like
a dog when the roller went on and it took some time to get her up,
but she never bucked. Every time the roller went on she sat down,
and we waited until madam was ready to continue. So never be
surprised at what a horse can get up to (or down to for that matter!).

50

Fig 29  Charles Coldrey and Karen Dudley had just put the roller on this bay colt (1988) by Fairy King, ex Mullaghroe, owned by Mr D.I. Russell and to be trained by Sir Mark Prescott BT., when Anthony Reynolds arrived with his camera. While expressing outrage at the feel of the roller, the colt must be kept going forward. Karen is just cracking the whip behind him.

Fig 30  Both handlers are behind the movement of the horse, giving him no chance of spinning round. Note all four feet off the ground. He almost looks as if he is about to perform a Capriole.

Fig 31  He is thinking about turning inwards.

Fig 32  So the lunger walks towards him to keep him
on the boards.

Fig 33   He gives a final buck.

Fig 34   And moves off around the lunge ring, starting to accept the roller.

Fig 35 The handlers, well positioned to keep him going correctly.

## TIGHTENING THE ROLLER

When he is really settled make him walk and halt on the boards. Go out to him again, reward him with praise and pats and both of you standing as you did before, tighten the roller so that it will not slip. It is going to stay in position for the next three or four days. He will be highly suspicious, so tighten up the roller gently. Once again, be prepared for fireworks as he moves off and feels the tighter girth. He will probably buck and then, more quickly than before, settle down to a good, rhythmical trot. Once he is nicely settled, stop him again (on the boards, of course) and, before you take him in, make sure that the pad and roller are firmly and comfortably in place. Now lead him back to his box and there take off the boots and cavesson leaving him wearing his headcollar and the roller. This will stay on until we are sure that he has become completely used to it and no longer notices that it is there.

# GROOMING

At this stage, two people should be on hand for grooming. Do not tie the horse up but have him held in case he jumps around. The handler must be on the same side as the person grooming so that he can swing the hindquarters away from the groomer by bringing the head towards himself. Yearlings can be a bit jumpy after rollering. Some take no notice and others worry for a day or two. Just occasionally we have had one worry so much as to give himself colic on the day he was rollered. We do not take the roller off straight away. If the animal has been difficult to roller and you take it off it is twice as difficult to get it back on because he knows what is coming. So leave it until he will lie down with it on and he is happy to live with it. If you think he will chew it or try to get it off, put a bib on him. Then, after three or four days' exercise, you can take it off.

Next day, put it on again at the start of his exercise in the lunge ring. Do not put it on in the box this time – it is better to be safe than sorry. It is much easier to get squashed or kicked in the box than in the lunge ring as you cannot get out of the way so easily. Once he has accepted it without demur you can put it on in the box. With experienced staff the roller will be patted and moved about on the horse's back while he is being groomed. On the first day or two he will need to be held and not tied up while this is done. As soon as he accepts it the roller is taken off for grooming and then put on again, so that he becomes accustomed to it being taken off and put back. If you are worried about this, wait a bit longer or get someone experienced to help. At this stage of training you will continue to lunge him for a few days. Side reins can go on as soon as possible.

---

### Watch Point

When the side reins are put on, the horse may put his head down. This pulls at the roller which may make him buck or bronc. Be warned in case this happens.

---

# SIDE REINING

Side reining is not difficult but the side reins do provide the first contact with the horse's mouth. As usual, settle him down before

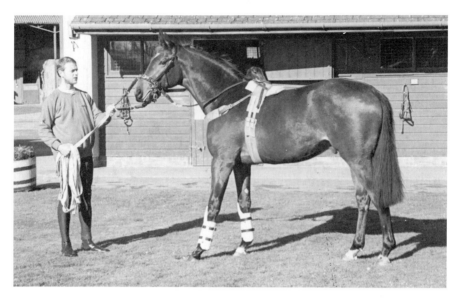

Fig 36   Prost (USA) (1987) bay colt, by Raise A Cup, ex
Wrap It Up, owned by Mrs P.L. Yong and trained by Bill
O'Gorman, with Sep Phrogg who has prepared him in
roller and side reins.

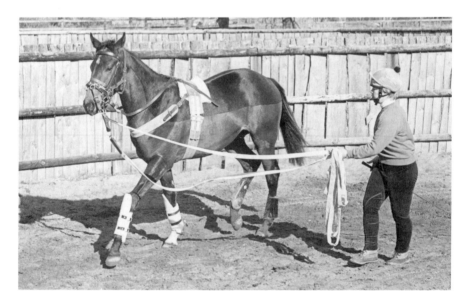

Fig 37   Tropic Power being lunged in side reins attached
to the roller.

advancing him to the next stage. There are two kinds of reins – plain leather and elasticated. We do not have them at all tight at this stage and either variety can be used. The side reins are attached to the rings of the bit, across the horse's wither and onto the opposite ring of the roller. The purposes of side reins are:

1. To get the feel of contact on the horse's mouth with the bit.
2. To encourage him to relax his head, neck and mouth.
3. To help maintain a constant and correct head carriage.

We do not use side reins from the bit to the girth as this does not produce a natural head carriage, rather a forced artificial collection breaking at the poll. Also, if the reins get too low, the yearling could get a foreleg caught up and break his jaw.

There is one more thing to accomplish before your horse is put into the tack. This is to accustom him to something like a lunge rein touching his hocks. What we do is to plait a length of rope (from old

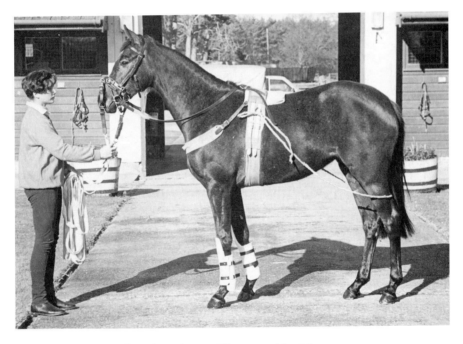

Fig 38   Ma Petite Chou (1987) grey filly, owned by Mrs
H.H. Morriss and trained by Geoff Wragg with Sharon
Seager. Note the string.

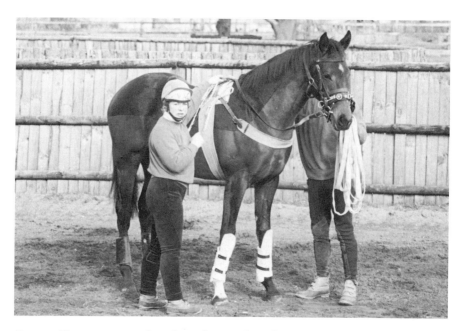

Fig 39   The string is tied to the roller on the off side and gently put over the horse's back.

Fig 40   It is then fed through the ring on the roller on the near side.

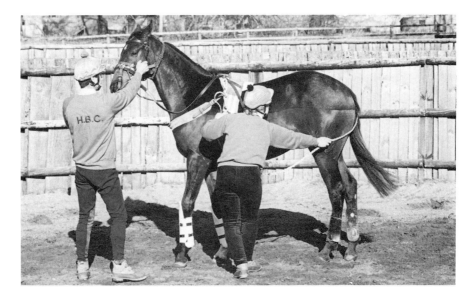

Fig 41 The string goes around behind the tail, the length is adjusted and a quick-release knot tied at the ring of the roller.

Fig 42 And away he goes, getting used to the string before putting the rein round him. If he is going to kick and resist, now is when it usually happens.

bale twine) and tie this from the girth ring of the roller around the horse's quarters and back to the girth ring on the opposite side. In case he kicks, put boots on behind. Now lunge him for a day or two with this and, once he has settled, you are ready to start long reining.

---

### Watch Point

Always have someone holding the horse when putting the string or rein round for the first time, as the horse will quite often try to run forward away from what he thinks is chasing him. **Do not** allow this. He must be completely settled at the walk, still being led, before lungeing can start again. Otherwise he can get a bit of a fright if you let him rush off and start bucking and kicking. The string will probably break too, which is a nuisance as you have to start again.

NB You must tie the string on with a quick-release knot so that you can get it off in a hurry if things go wrong, such as the horse getting one leg outside the string if he is naughty.

---

## SHOEING

Some yearlings come in for starting with front shoes on and some without. If they have no shoes on, we get the fronts put on immediately after they have been rollered. Under no circumstances must hind shoes be put on until after the horse has been ridden away. This is in case you get kicked while driving in the long reins or he kicks himself.

# 5

# Long Reins

Driving in long reins is a very important part of the starting process. Horses who are broken without going in the reins are never quite as good. They do not carry themselves as well and can be picked out of a string a mile away. The salient advantages of long reining are:

1. The horse gets used to the feel of the reins on his side and so does not resent the rider's legs when he is first ridden.
2. The horse gets accustomed to the feel of the reins around his hocks and becomes much less nervous about having his hind legs touched, learning not to kick at anything, especially people and other horses.
3. Long reining is the first stage in teaching a horse to steer. The driver has direct contact, through the reins, to the horse's mouth and can move the horse sideways by using the reins against his side. Just as the rider's hands indicate direction and speed, so do the driver's reins; just as the rider creates impulsion and controls the swing of the quarters with his legs, so does the driver with the reins against the horse's side. It is much easier for the horse to learn to steer without the rider's weight.
4. In the long rein the horse will feel the driver's hands in contact through the bit. Impulsion will be created as the driver gets behind the horse and almost immediately the horse will start to carry himself. It is this carriage of head, neck and body that identifies the well-started horse.
5. Above all these points, the most important benefit of long reining is that it makes a horse brave. He is facing the world on his own, with the driver encouraging him from behind. Well handled, he will soon get used to traffic and noises in hedges, and will learn to face anything which is placed in his path. As you can see from the pictures, our yearlings go all over the place in the reins and soon become completely self-confident.

Although it is perfectly possible to start a horse in the reins on your own, it is always advisable to have a helper, especially with a horse who you think could be awkward.

## REINS

It is important to hold the reins correctly and to be comfortable with them. First attach them to a hook in the tack room or somewhere suitable to practice.

**Left Rein**   Drop the reins on the ground. Stand on the near side of the horse facing the head, your right shoulder to his shoulder. Hold the left rein in your right hand under the bit and loop the rest of the rein on the ground into your right hand. Transfer all the looped rein into your left hand.

**Right Rein**   Take the right rein under the bit and into your left hand using the first finger of your left hand to keep the two reins separated. Loop the right rein into your left hand until looped up tidily. Then separate the two bundles of reins and put them round the horse as shown in the photographs.

Fig 43   This photograph shows how the reins and side reins are fitted.

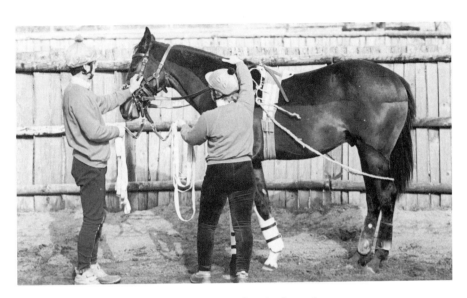

Fig 44 Passing the right outside rein under the horse's neck to your right hand over the neck. Take care not to pass the rein through the side rein, otherwise the lunge rein will be trapped inside the side rein.

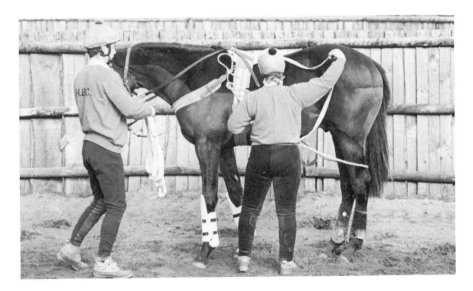

Fig 45 In all these photographs, note the total concentration of everyone taking part. This is vital for safety and is one of the great lessons learnt from working with these young Thoroughbreds. In this case, the helper is holding the left rein while the driver puts the right rein over the quarters.

Fig 46  As the driver takes the right rein around the back, her helper hands her the left rein, still holding the horse's head until the driver is ready to start. This picture perfectly illustrates the value of using the string behind the hocks before you start with the long reins.

Fig 47  The helper has moved away and the driver now has the horse going nicely forward in the reins.

Throughout the starting process we have always repeated the last lesson before starting a new one. In this case, lunge the horse with a string around the hocks first. As soon as he settles, you are ready to go on. Now change the fixing of the lunge reins so that they buckle onto the rings of the snaffle **below** the side reins with the bit connector below that.

## PUTTING THE REIN ROUND

Get your helper to hold the horse's head and the left rein, while you pass the right rein under the horse's neck to your right hand which is over the horse's neck. Then pass the rein over the animal's back and along towards the tail until it drops down on to the hocks, taking care not to let it get too long or drop too low. Do not get cow kicked! Fillies are apt to try you out at this point.

As before, have the horse led round the lunge ring (to the left, of course) to avoid him running away from the rein. You must hold the right rein round the horse while he walks round the ring until he is settled, well out of kicking distance. Keeping the equal-sided triangle position that we described in Chapter 3, carry on just as if you were lungeing but with the left rein in your left hand and the right rein around the back of the horse into your right hand. The helper drops away and you have the horse on your own in the reins. Watch that the helper does not get run over by the reins. You can walk and trot in the lunge ring and change the rein by gradually falling in behind the horse, steering him across the ring and going off the other way as you approach the wall, in a half figure of eight.

---

**Watch Point**

When changing direction, do not forget to shorten the rein asking for direction and lengthen the other one to allow the horse to turn his head into the direction being asked for. If you do not, you will confuse and upset the horse, muddle him and, most important, make it physically impossible for him to turn. If you get it really wrong he can only rear or go backwards. Practise first on an old pony. It soon becomes second nature.

---

65

Fig 48 Changing the rein, across the middle of the ring. Notice how the new inside rein is working just like the inside leg of a rider against the horse's side with the outside rein allowing the head to be bent in the direction he is now going.

If you have a particularly difficult animal, it is as well to keep him at walk inside the reins for several minutes with your helper preventing him from rushing off and trying to run away. Normally you will have very little trouble if you have already lunged with the string on.

---

### Watch Point

When you change the rein, for the first few times some will run away from the long rein touching him the other side. Be ready for this so that you do not jerk the horse in the mouth. Just go forward with him until he is settled in the other direction. If he persists in being difficult through the change, halt in the centre of the ring and quietly cross behind him before moving off. If necessary, have him held and then led through the turn. They soon accept this.

---

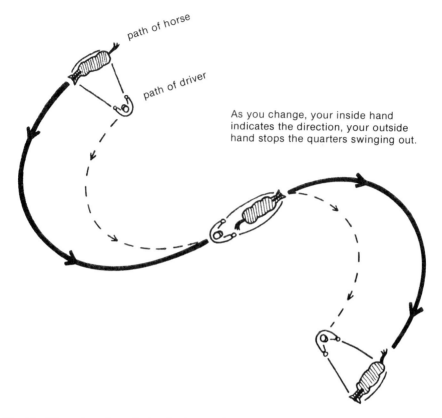

path of horse

path of driver

As you change, your inside hand indicates the direction, your outside hand stops the quarters swinging out.

Fig 49   Changing the rein in the lunge ring.

As you change, your inside hand indicates the direction, your outside hand stops the quarters swinging out. Once your horse has settled down and is doing this nicely, stop. The whole starting process is hugely demanding on his body and mind. Never go on too long. Be content with work well done each day and be very careful if he starts to be difficult or inattentive. This is usually a sign that you have gone on for too long. Always try and finish your work on a good note. (This last rule applies throughout a horse's life.)

## TACKING UP

Once all is going well in the reins it is time to substitute the saddle for the roller. This can be done in the stable. Put on the cavesson with

Fig 50   Debbie Kay shows Star of Italy (1988) brown colt
by Superlative, ex Arianna Aldini, owned by Mr B. Haggas
and trained by Sir Mark Prescott, BT., tacked up with reins
in the lungeing position.

reins in the lunge position, not on the bit rings. Take off the roller
(girth first then the breast strap) and put on a breastplate. Then put
your stable rubber and numnah on his back, one person holding the
horse and one person tacking up. Place a light race exercise saddle
carefully but firmly over the numnah, talking to him confidently all
the while. Next fasten the breastplate and tighten the girth sufficiently to keep it in place. Finally, put on the side reins exactly as
before, crossed over the withers, not too tight, and buckled to the
extension from the girth.

Now, although you should not get it, be ready for the same
reaction you got when your horse first felt the roller. As he moves
forward, the unaccustomed weight on his back might make his back
go up. Do not allow this. Discipline with the voice and top lunge rein
on the cavesson. Walk him round the box to let him feel the saddle
moving about. Then change the reins back to drive and drive him to
the lunge ring, being led at the same time. If he decides to be silly you
have a helper.

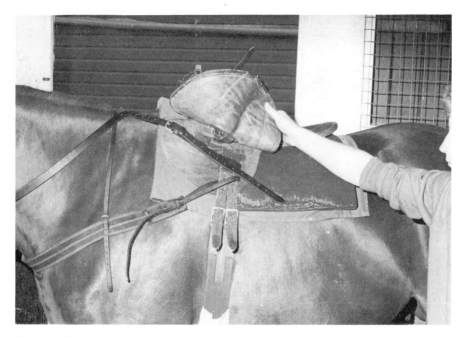

Fig 51  This photograph illustrates how the side reins
are connected to the saddle and the breastplate around both
girth straps. (Buckle guard removed for the purposes of
photography.)

---

**Watch Point**

If he has been quiet up till now, he may have a bit of a buck
when he starts trotting and feels the saddle. Do not worry –
let him. Better now than when the rider gets on! If you have
got your timing right and assessed your horse correctly this
should not happen.

---

Do not take the reins from the bit through the rings on the roller or
through the stirrups to the hands. Our reins run directly from the
bit to the driver's hands.

We normally rug-up our yearlings once they have been driven in
the tack. Very rarely at this stage do we get any reaction. The horses
simply accept it as part of their routine. We do, however, put the
roller, with breastplate, on over the top of the rug for a couple of
days to stop them pulling it off over their heads (some Houdini colts

Fig 52   What happens when the rein is passed through a
stirrup on its way from the horse's mouth to the driver's
hand. If the horse goes backwards, the rein pulls him back
even more.

think this a great game and it can become expensive in rug repairs!)
and of course you do not want the rug to frighten the horse if it slips
during the night. Always have a helper. We put the rugs on when
there are staff about in case of accidents, not just before lunch hour
or last thing at night. Putting the rug on at this stage makes backing
easier as the horse gets used to the rug going on and off. It actually
makes quite a difference to nervous animals. On no account take off
the headcollar until he is completely used to the rug. Otherwise if it
slips or if he takes fright you are going to have a terrible job trying to
catch him and put things right.

You can see from Fig 52 that if the reins are put through the
stirrups and the horse tries to run round or run backwards away
from you, the stirrup will act as a lever. The more you hold on and
try to stop the horse, the more you end up pulling him away from
you. The same applies when you take the rein over a horse's head
when he is wearing a running or bib martingale. If he is startled and
runs back, you end up pulling him backwards instead of stopping
him. You can work this out by putting a running martingale on an old

horse or pony in the box. Take the reins over the head with the martingale attached to the girth and study the action of the reins through the rings – a pulley! It is interesting to note that this method of having the reins direct from the hands to the horse's mouth is the one used with the Lippizaners at the Spanish Riding School in Vienna. This supports our claim that our methods are classic methods which should be used for all horses.

# DRIVING

The first few times that you drive your horse in the ring, lead him back to his box. But once he is happy and going calmly you can get your helper back again to open the gate and walk beside him while you drive him out of the lunge ring and back into his box. Start in the

Fig 53   Driving out of the lunge ring to face the outside world for the first time. Notice the front boots — these are Porter boots, which give excellent protection if a horse should go down on his knees. As you can see, they are suspended from below and so provide a pad on which the horse will kneel if, by any chance, he falls over.

Fig 54 Gloplug, by Kalglow, ex State Pension, owned by
Hugh and Pat McCalmont, returns sweetly to her box.
Note Emily Vickerman is standing by, ready to help if
needed.

Fig 55 Next time, Gloplug is driven straight out from her
box.

Fig 56  John Hernon and Stephen Ballantyne were two
stalwart members of our 1989/90 team. Here, they are
taking out Tina's Pet, ex City Lake Lass trained by Sir
Mark Prescott, BT., in the reins outside the lunge ring for
the first time.

lunge ring but when he is ready drive him out, gradually increasing
the work until you can take him for a drive along tracks and quiet
roads, through woods, around trees, past houses and vehicles, up
and down hills and through gateways, standing to open the gates.
Practise trotting figures of eight, which you start in the lunge ring
and continue outside when you are confident. It can be done in a
small paddock at walk to start with. It is great fun and gives the
driver a terrific sense of achievement as the horse glides through the
change of direction. This takes a bit of practice. Do not be caught
flat-footed or you might suddenly find yourself and the yearling
going faster than you expected or intended, and always drive him
back into his box at the end. Until you are very confident, and always
on public roads, it is advisable to have a helper with you who needs
to do nothing except be there in case you get into difficulty and to
control the traffic. It is very important not to frighten the horse. It is

Fig 57 Driving a 'serpentine' down a line of trees. It teaches suppleness and bravery as the horse learns to go anywhere and do anything.

Fig 58 Lovely change of bend. The horse must always look in the direction he is going.

Fig 59   He is beautifully relaxed, bending correctly and
taking a great interest in what he is doing.

Fig 60   Note throughout this sequence that the side reins
are never so tight as to prevent the horse having freedom
of his head and neck in all normal positions.

Figs 61 and 62   As the horse gets more confident in the
long reins he can be taught more complicated things. Here
he is learning to stand and wait and move on quietly when
opening and closing a gate. Both reins in the right hand
leaving the left hand free to open the gate. Victoria keeps
her eyes on the horse, not on the gate, so she can anticipate any trouble and so prevent it happening.

Fig 63   This good horse (Tropic Power) has learned to
stand and wait while Victoria moves away from him.

Fig 64   When she is ready he willingly walks on, looking
keenly ahead to see what new excitements the world has
in store. Note the right rein has too big a loop and might
trip up the driver if she is unaware of it — this is corrected
in the next picture.

Fig 65   Before Tropic
Power can go on he
must, like all good
countrymen, shut the
gate behind him. All our
gates have these loops of
rope so that, during the
day, it is easy to open
and shut them while
mounted.

Fig 66   A string of yearlings driven through the village of Herringswell.

Fig 67   It is advisable to take helpers with you when driving on public roads. This sort of exercise is an ideal way to get the horses used to the big wide world.

Fig 68  Now they are alongside each other — learning to change position, go close behind another horse and take the lead. All this helps to make them independent and prepares them to take their own line.

better for your horse to be led past anything new and alarming for the first time so that he never loses confidence. Always remember to praise him when he has done well.

The period of long reining gets the drivers incredibly fit. They will run behind a trotting horse uphill for a mile without drawing breath and by the end of the starting season are hard, lean and exhausted. We often take the yearlings out in groups so that they get used to working with other horses and give each other confidence. When we do, though, we always have a few helpers walking alongside to prevent any problems occurring. It is a lovely sight to see a string of beautiful thoroughbred yearlings being driven through the village. When they are out walking we make them change places and go upsides with one another and, when walking across the field, go in line abreast so that they learn to take their own line. It always seems to us a bad lesson to teach racehorses that the one thing they must not do is overtake the horse in front!

# 6

# Backing and Riding Away

## BACKING

Backing starts during the period when the horse is being driven in the long reins. After about a week in the reins (it is impossible to be specific with these timings as all horses are different and the time to move forward is one that experience alone will teach you), you will drive the horse back into his box and decide that he is ready for someone to lean over him. This is a three-person operation. You will

Fig 69   Ridden with full tack and cavesson. Melanie Birchall riding Sanctorum by Habitat, ex Sancta, owned by Lord Howard de Walden and trained by Henry Cecil.

Fig 70   Stuart Walton leans over Sir Gordon White's 1988 colt, by Diesis, ex Informatique. Always lean over and back the horse in the box to start with. When he is used to the feel of a rider on his back, you can mount in the lunge ring in exactly the same way.

need to hold the horse's head (with the long reins back in the lungeing position) while your helper legs up the jockey. You want a very lightweight person for this last job – ours are usually around seven stone.

The first time you do it you should leg the jockey up to lean across the horse's withers, but he should not stay up, even for a second. The jockey bends his left leg at the knee, the legger-up lifts him up over the withers and immediately lets him down again, and up again and down again several times until you say, 'Right, stay up next time'. Then the jockey is left leaning over the withers. While he is up there he should be praising the horse and patting and handling him boldly on his neck, shoulder and rib-cage. Make sure that the horse has seen the jockey, otherwise he will jump when he sits up.

After a minute or two the exercise is repeated and, if there is no serious reaction, you can move the jockey back to lean over

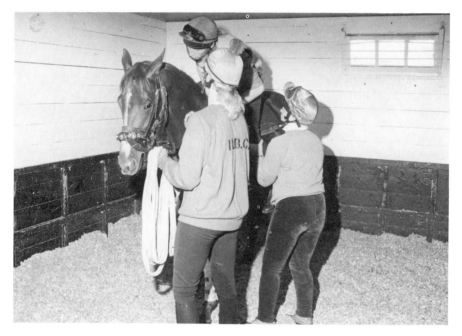

Fig 71 Getting up very lightly in the saddle.

the saddle. When the horse is quite used to this you can give the command 'Walk On' and lead the horse around the box two or three times. This ought to be repeated for a couple of days and when you are ready the jockey can start to sit in the saddle. The procedure is the same as for leaning over. You leg up your jockey who is off again before his seat has done more than just lightly rest in the saddle and so it goes on for two or three times until you tell him to stay up again. This time he should sit lightly in the saddle.

## RIDING AWAY

Once the horse is accepting this you can walk on round the box with the jockey riding and gradually, over a period of a couple of days, making the horse aware of and accepting his legs. Both when leaning over and when riding around the box you should start to the left and go on to do a little bit in either direction. Before you or the horse know it he is being ridden in the box and ready to be 'ridden away'. A good large box should be used – 16 × 16ft (5 × 5m). A lunge ring is too

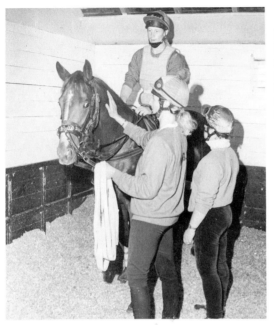

Fig 72 You can see from his eye that the colt is not yet quite happy, but everyone is reassuring him that there is nothing to worry about and very soon ...

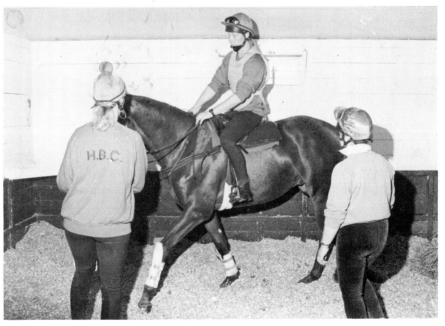

Fig 73 ... he is walking happily round the box. In these four pictures, notice the lack of tension in all of the people concerned, especially how light a feel Stuart has on the reins.

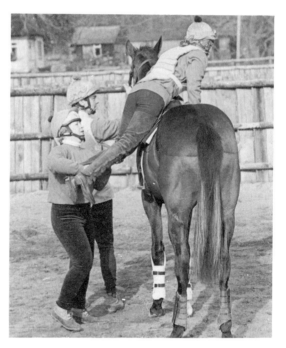

Fig 74 Victoria and Charles Coldrey with Anita Hall backing Tropic Power. Anita backed 100 yearlings and two-year-olds in the winter of 1989/90.

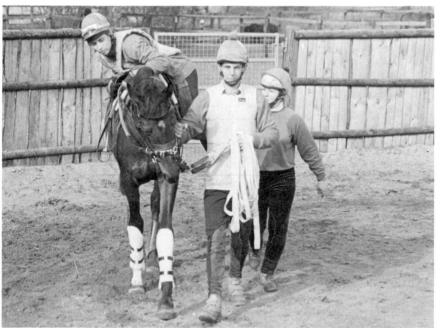

Fig 75 Leaning over to get him used to the rider's weight.

Fig 76   Now, sitting in the saddle, Anita accustoms the horse to her weight in the saddle, contact through the reins and gradually, to the rider's leg.

Fig 77   Now, ridden around the lunge ring on lunge reins, Tropic Power is ready to go loose. He is still keeping an eye on the lunger in case anything untoward occurs. As Monty Roberts would say, he and Charles are still 'joined up'.

big, as the animal will expect to trot and he could get going and buck the jockey off. In his stable he will only expect to walk, so he will.

The next stage is to back the horse outside and we do this in the lunge ring. The procedure is just the same. First you take him for a short drive in the reins, then you drive him back into the box and ride him round the box, before driving him out to the lunge ring. Your team of three starts leaning over and walking on and then the jockey sits in the saddle. When the horse has walked and trotted calmly the helper fades out of the picture so that you have the ridden horse on the lunge at walk and trot in both directions. When you think he is ready and it is safe to do so, undo the long reins and take them off while you are walking beside the horse. Now you too can fade away to the centre of the ring and the horse can be ridden around it free. Whenever you finish riding, let the jockey get on and off several times to make sure that the horse does not resent this.

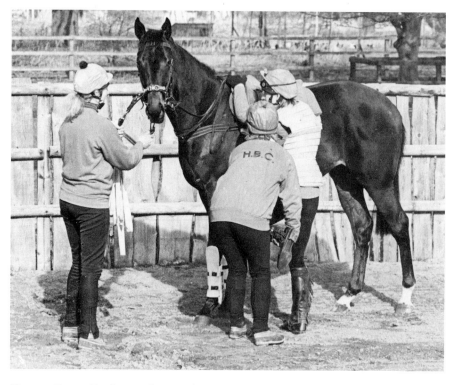

Fig 78   Karen Dudley with Teresa Ellwood and Stuart Walton backing Star of Italy.

Fig 79   Sitting lightly in the saddle.

Fig 80   Everyone concentrating, including Star of Italy.

Fig 81 He is now ready to go loose, so Karen will take off the reins.

Fig 82 And off he goes around the ring. Teresa has stayed in the ring to make sure that he goes forward and stays on the boards.

---

### Watch Point

In all the photographs you can see that all members of the team are wearing proper crash hats, correctly fastened, and that the jockey has a back protector. Please do not let anyone argue about this. Not to wear these safety aids is silly and selfishly arrogant.

---

The first time you ride a horse outside the ring it is better for him to be led (known in Newmarket as 'rode and led'). We have a totally enclosed 4-furlong all-weather canter and, once you are satisfied that it is safe to do so, you can slip the lunge reins and let him off to be ridden on his own. It is a good idea to have a steady old lead horse on hand to lead the young, newly started horse. This will give him

Fig 83  'I'm a bit camera-shy, and anyway this is not my best side'. Star of Italy the first time he was on the all-weather canter.

Fig 84  The sudden freedom has gone to his head and he is having a bit of fun – as is Stuart.

Fig 85  Tropic Power and Star of Italy soon settle down to their work.

Fig 86  They walk past the camera like a couple of experienced horses.

confidence and help you to achieve your three objectives at this stage of training. They are:

1. To go forward.
2. To go straight.
3. To go calmly.

---

### Watch Point

Do not take a newly backed yearling somewhere he has not been before. It is only asking for trouble. All our yearlings are driven round the canter before being ridden on it so all the spooks have been dealt with before the jockey appears. You must not ask a yearling to cope with too many new things at once.

---

# 7

# The Follow-Up and Cantering

Let us say that so far we have taken three weeks and that we are planning to complete the starting process and have a well-mannered horse, going correctly and calmly and looking good, in six weeks. The pressure of time is always there, for various reasons. One is the cost to the owner. In the case of racehorses this is immaterial because the horse will cost the same after the starting is done, but for someone

Fig 87   Superforce (1988) bay colt by Superlative, ex Loup de Mer, owned by Mrs P.L. Yong and trained by Bill O'Gorman. Here ridden by Niamh Nash in normal tack, the cavesson now replaced by a Fulmer snaffle.

who has sent in a horse just to be started and returned, an extra two weeks can mean a hefty increase. Another reason is foolish pride. The sooner people understand that there is nothing clever in rushing the job just so that you can boast about how quickly it was done, the better it will be for the unfortunate horses. A third reason is the feeling that owners will think that you are not getting on with the job if they do not see rapid progress being made.

Our experience is that if you take the trouble to explain what you are doing and why, owners will understand and be content if you find that their horse needs a little extra time. You cannot do this job properly to a timetable. Some horses are mentally and physically able to take much more than others and you can go more quickly with them. Others will get hung up at a particular stage and you will simply have to give them a few days longer. It makes no difference whatsoever in the long run. Horses tell you when they are ready and, just as it is wrong to go too fast, it is equally wrong not to make steady advances. Young horses get bored and stale very easily and it is essential to keep their attention and interest at every stage of

Fig 88   Young horses get bored and stale very easily and it is essential to keep their attention and interest at every stage of training.

training. With the pressure on us of more horses waiting to come in for starting, it is clearly important not to waste time but to get them ridden away as soon as possible to make room for the next intake.

## THE FOLLOW-UP

Once a young horse is ridden away his horizons are greatly enlarged. We know what we are trying to achieve – forward, straight, calm – but we need to think about how to achieve these goals most easily. It is here that a bit of horse psychology is required. It is the next three or four weeks that set the horse's attitude towards his work. If he enjoys it, finds it interesting, does not get exhausted but feels well and happy, the end product will be a much better one.

Even mature horses find it difficult to concentrate for long periods. The attention span of a yearling or two-year-old is no more than a few minutes, so the best method of teaching is for them to learn without knowing they have been taught.

We do not keep our pupils in the formal surroundings of the all-weather circuit for too long. We spend just a couple of days riding around the track, very often with one or two others at the same stage and preferably with an old lead horse to set a good example in front. During these days the youngsters will do short distances of around two or three furlongs at a steady canter. This can be increased gradually to four furlongs, which on our track is one circuit. You will be amazed at how quickly the horses strengthen up and learn to carry themselves and go straight.

The next stage is to take them away from the track. We always settle them down on the track first and, after a steady trot for a mile or so, take them out behind the leader on to the quiet roads, tracks and woods nearby. A good lead horse is a huge advantage. If he just plods past alarming things like tractors and does not shy when pigeons suddenly bash about in the bushes, the young starter will plod along behind him and will soon become good and safe in traffic. Whatever you do, do not get young horses tired. They must enjoy their work at all costs, and getting them exhausted is a sure way of browning them off. Never forget that they cannot take much yet, either mentally or physically.

So, off you go behind your lead horse. Lightweight jockeys are essential, ideally with strong legs and light hands. Our well-started yearlings or two-year-olds will have developed a good head-carriage

Fig 89  If your lead horse just plods past alarming things
like tractors and does not shy when pigeons suddenly bash
about in the bushes, the young starter will plod along
behind him.

in the long reins and there is no reason why they should not keep this
when they are ridden. They must keep going forward. It is when
they drop the bit and the jockey is left with nothing in his hands that
things go wrong.

Do not go too far at first and vary the ride as much as possible from
day to day. The best way of teaching a horse to turn and to bend
around your inside leg is to ride amongst and around trees. Accompany this with use of the correct aids, and in no time you will find
that you have taught him to associate the aids with the movements
and will do what you want without the trees to help. As the horses
settle down, make them go through gaps between trees and then,
perhaps, stand still between two trees – their first training for the
starting stalls. Use the land and the facilities that you have at your
disposal to the best advantage. Always think how you can keep your
horses interested and enjoying their work. If you use your imagin-
ation you can teach them an amazing amount, making it real fun
for both horses and jockeys. Do not forget to make all the horses that
you start take the lead at some time each day. In this way they will

learn to face the world on their own. You can sometimes get a racehorse so used to following another one all the time that if he hits the front he stops dead in his tracks. It all comes down to these vital early stages in training.

## BASIC RULES

1.   Always work your horses in both directions. When they are on the racecourse they must be able to gallop either way equally easily. We have seen that they are naturally one-sided, so they have to become ambidextrous. Do not forget that the difference between immortality and oblivion for a horse can be as little as eighteen inches over a mile and a half. Change legs twice unnecessarily and you have lost it. Anything that we can do to help improve performance by this minute margin must be done.

2.   When trotting make your jockeys ride on the correct diagonal. If they do not, the horse's back muscles will develop more on one side than the other and he will not be even-handed. Do not scoff at this – it is actually very important and, even if you do not believe us, it costs nothing and can only do good.

3.   Do not let your horse stop of his own accord. Forward movement is the single most important factor in the initial training of all horses. We put our old lead horse in front to keep the young ones going forward. If you are in a string and the horse in front of you balks and stops, ride past – first to give him a lead and second to keep your own horse going forward.

4.   Think forward. The whole attitude of the rider must be forward. At walk, trot and canter keep your horse going forward; look ahead and not down and let your horse swing along under you from a strong leg, a light seat and a sensitive hand. Some racing lads have the appalling habit of moving both hands simultaneously from side to side in the extraordinary hope that this makes the horse go forward. It does not; it simply helps to desensitise the mouth of a muddled horse.

## THE CANTER

A week or two of riding out like this will bring the horse on amazingly. If you are lucky enough to have a safe track with good,

Fig 90   Do not let your jockeys stop to shorten their
stirrups.

level going there is no reason why you should not let your horses
have a canter – they will absolutely love it and will nearly always
follow the lead horse calmly and happily. Let it not be a formal canter
with lots of preparation that lets them know in advance that something different is coming up. Do not, for example, let your jockeys
stop and shorten their stirrups. This is a sure way of getting your
horse unnecessarily worked up. Rather, as you come to a suitable
place let them roll on into canter and pull up to trot and then walk
when you think they have done enough. It is not necessary to
emulate the top jockeys just to go for a hack canter!

In this way you should have given your horse an excellent start. He
should by now be physically much stronger (it is absolutely amazing
to watch the metamorphosis from foal to racehorse in just a few
weeks). Whether you are starting a racehorse or not is immaterial.
Everything we have written so far applies equally to all horses
whatever their *métier*. Your horse should now give you a good ride
fulfilling our objectives of going forward, straight and calmly at all
paces. A final word of advice from Xenophon:

The one great precept and practice in using a horse is this
– never deal with him when you are in a fit of passion. A
fit of passion is a thing that has no foresight in it, and so
we often have to rue the day when we gave way to it.
Consequently, when your horse shies at an object and is
unwilling to go up to it, he should be shown that there is
nothing fearful in it, least of all to a courageous horse like
him; but if this fails, touch the object yourself that seems
so dreadful to him, and lead him up to it with gentleness.
Compulsion and blows inspire only the more fear; for
when horses are hurt at such a time, they think that what
they shied at is the cause of the hurt.

# PART 2

# FURTHER PROGRESS

# 8

# Keeping Your Young Horse Well

The factors that affect the wellbeing of a horse are: feeding, worms, teeth, feet, work, aches and pains, and contentment.

## FEEDING

Other things being equal, it is work that makes a horse look strong and well and not what he eats. You can fill a horse with good food and he will still not look right unless he is doing the right sort of work. And the food must be most carefully related to the amount of work done.

During the starting process, the last thing that you want is a horse who is above himself, so do not feed too much hard food until he has been ridden away and is settling down. However, plenty of good hay is essential. The quality of your hay is the single most important factor in feeding.

Once our horses are being ridden every day we start to step up the feed, keeping a very careful eye on how each horse is going and how he is behaving. We work on the principle of giving them as much of the best-quality feed as we can without getting them misbehaving. We mash on Wednesday and Saturday nights unless they are competing or working seriously the next day. This is an excellent thing for the digestion.

## WORMS

Unless we know that a very strict worming programme has been carried out and is up to date, we worm the young horses for starting, soon after they arrive, using Eqvalan. Thereafter, we worm once a month alternating with two other good wormers so as to cover a broad spectrum of parasites.

# TEETH

We have always said of a thin horse who will not thrive, 'If it isn't worms, it's teeth.' We did mention teeth, as they apply to yearlings, in Chapter 2, but horses of all ages need their teeth regularly checked, especially in the years before they have a full mouth, which they get at five years of age. If you are not sure how to check the teeth yourself (it is very easy and something you should ask your vet to teach you), get your vet to look at them for you. You are looking for good flat, grinding surfaces. If the sides of the teeth are ridged and sharp the horse will be unable to chew his food properly and will not be able to make the best use of it. Added to this, if it actually hurts to eat, he will not eat up, thereby wasting your money and continuing to look poor.

Horses lose their milk teeth between three and five years. Sometimes they do not come out easily and are extremely uncomfortable. We have had cases where they become quite deeply embedded in the side of the gum which is really very painful. Certainly, they are irritating enough to make the horse stop eating and to be a miserable ride, unwilling or unable to accept the bit and throwing his head about in an effort to escape the discomfort. Very often you can take these caps off with your fingers, but not always, and in such cases your vet can do it very easily with a pair of pincers he will have for the purpose. A sign that a horse needs these milk teeth caps removed is horrible smelly breath which results from decaying food lodging between the old and new teeth. Good teeth are a major factor in achieving and maintaining good conditions.

## Wolf Teeth

We often have to remove wolf teeth. Some vets may tell you that taking them out does not make any difference but we believe that this is quite wrong. If you ever have a horse with a mouth problem, if he is throwing his head about, carrying it to one side, pulling, will not accept the bit or is in any way uncomfortable in his mouth, look and see if he has got wolf teeth. If he has, ask your vet to take them out. You will be amazed at the result. We have even heard of a dealer who went round looking for horses who were going badly. He used to look in their mouths and if they had wolf teeth he bought them, had the teeth out and was able to sell them as reformed characters immediately thereafter. We have certainly had many difficult horses who have been absolutely transformed by this simple operation.

## FEET

Feet are vitally important. Our farrier, Mark Rose, is an expert who is always conscious of the importance of balance. His apprentice, Darren Rose (no relation), has just passed his Diploma of the Worshipful Company of Farriers and is now fully qualified. With Mark's agreement, Darren has written a piece for us which is reproduced as Appendix 2.

Whatever the farrier does to keep the feet right and to correct imbalance, it is a top priority to keep them clean. In our experience you are less likely to get foot problems on shavings than on straw.

## WORK

Not much more needs to be said about work than we have already written. The older a horse gets, the more work he can take and the more quickly he can be got fit. Never get to the bottom of a young horse. They can be ruined in one day. What they do want is consistency and a few simple rules:

1. No fast work on a Monday (if Sunday has been a rest day) or after any period of enforced rest. One bad effect of disregarding this is Setfast, which can be difficult to rectify.
2. One easy day, for example a good longish piece of road work, in the middle of the week.
3. A really good exercise on Saturday, because they will rest on Sunday.
4. As they get fitter, increase the duration of the exercise as well as the intensity of it.
5. Try to get them out at the same time each day. Horses are creatures of habit and will fret if left in when they expect to go out.
6. Put as much variety into the work as possible to keep them interested and fresh in their outlook.

## ACHES AND PAINS

Horses get damned by riders and trainers for being useless, lazy, gutless, cowardly and so on when it is no fault of their own. There is really no such thing as a 'problem horse', only problem people, and we think that it is largely true to say that if a horse is not giving of his best according to his ability, there is almost certainly a physical reason. He cannot do what is wanted because it hurts.

When sports teams travel they never go anywhere without their physiotherapist. Yet athletes do not have someone sitting on their backs while they are running or jumping. Given that people have as much back trouble as they do, how much more likely is it that horses will suffer in the same way.

We find that a high proportion of the young horses who come to us, and almost 100 per cent of those who come in with the reputation of being no good, have a problem somewhere between their occipital axis, where the head and the spine join, and the sacro-iliac joint of the pelvis. We can usually identify the problem and our equitherapist, Carol Whitwood, comes once a week to check and treat the horses who have been put in the 'back book'. Her results are truly marvellous. Without doubt, she removes the aches and pains from very many horses and enables them to go back to competing as well as ever.

What we are trying to say is that if you have a horse who suddenly starts going below par, do not beat him or force him or get some fierce professional in to school him. Rather try to find out, with the help of your vet, if you can identify the problem yourself. Seek out the cause, get it put right and you will not have to resort to violence or force of any kind. After all these years we ought to have known better when one of our event horses, who had been going brilliantly, suddenly had six fences down in the show-jumping phase. We withdrew from the cross-country, took his temperature, examined him from head to foot and found nothing. We jumped him the next day with awful results. 'Heavens', I thought, 'We must get a show-jumping instructor to show us where we are going wrong'. Luckily the penny dropped and we checked his back. Carol Whitwood examined him and found aches and pains everywhere. She gave him one treatment followed by two or three days' rest and the next time out he was right back on form and gave us a splendid clear round. We now think that he must have been cast in his box and twisted his back badly trying to get up.

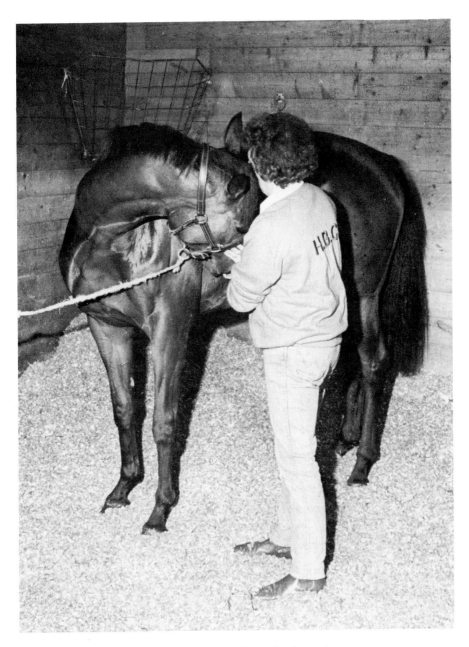

Fig 91 Carol Whitwood at work. Here she is checking the
poll to make sure that the horse can bend his head and
neck in each direction and without any pain.

Fig 92   Here, Carol is easing muscle spasm in the lumber
region of the back.

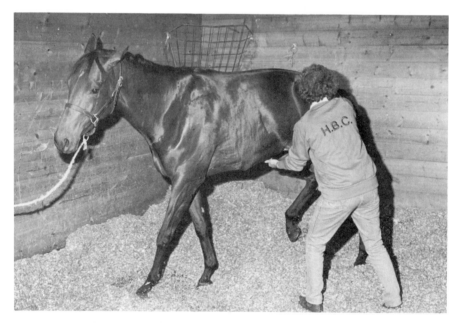

Fig 93   Here the horse is arching his back as Carol
tests for movement of the spine without pain.

As equitherapy is still, unfortunately, a matter for disbelief and even controversy in some circles, we have put the case, from a layman's point of view, separately in Appendix 1.

# CONTENTMENT

We touched on the subject of keeping horses happy in the Introduction. There is no doubt that contentment comes from the people with whom a horse is in contact. A cheerful, happy team produces cheerful happy horses. Here are just some of the things that help to keep a horse at ease:

**Deep, clean, dry bed**  This speaks for itself. We use wood shavings which are much quicker and easier, but more expensive than straw. We keep a few straw beds for horses with open wounds (e.g. after gelding) for which shavings are unsuitable. Other advantages of shavings are that they are free of anything that can adversely affect the horse's lungs and they are not edible.

Eating bedding is an infuriating habit as the horse cannot be got fit or slim if he has a gutful of straw.

**Unlimited clean, fresh water**  We do not use automatic drinkers as it is so often important to know how much a horse has drunk. We use white water buckets which show at a glance whether they and the water are clean and need filling.

**Regularity**  The stable should be run to a routine so that, except as dictated by having to compete, the horse knows what is going to happen and when. Regularity is a factor in getting horses to eat up and do well.

**Good grooming**  There is nothing that makes a horse feel better than his daily grooming. It is obvious that horses will feel and be better for being thoroughly clean but the actual grooming process itself is one that induces real contentment.

**Peace and quiet**  In the morning the yard is all bustle and go and all of the horses are exercised. Only in emergencies do we take horses out in the afternoon. That is the time when they are groomed and, as far as possible, the yard is kept fairly quiet so that the horses are relaxed and calm. We hate disturbing them after the evening feed. It is a magical time when you quietly go up to the yard in the evening, listen to the sounds of contented horses and creep away again without their knowing you were there.

**Calm staff**  You should never, well hardly ever, hear anyone shouting in a stable. If your team are on top of their job they will not have to get excited to make their horses behave themselves. Of course, you do occasionally get a horse who is really bad in his box and you must get one of your best staff members to deal with this. Colts must never be petted and fussed over. They can become overbearing and familiar. They must, in the interests of safety, be made to respect people. If they are properly brought up there will only very rarely be a problem. Fillies can be loved as much as you like and it only does them good.

This chapter is not out of place in this book. You cannot do well with horses who feel bad. When they feel good, they will give you their best and be a joy to train.

# 9

# The First Branch of the Tree – Racing

The starting process is now completed. By the end of about six weeks we should have achieved all our original objectives. Now we must prepare the horse to race. We need to get the horse ready for the trainer to start serious work. We are trying to achieve a sound, fairly fit, keen, enthusiastic and bold horse.

## A SOUND HORSE

It is not our job to gallop the horse, that is for the trainer, but if we get him three-quarters fit, the trainer can complete the job in the way that he wants it done. Flat racehorses are proverbially like glass.

Fig 94   Winter 1988/89. With a couple of exceptions, these are all two-year-olds started at Herringswell.

111

At their tender age they can be damaged terribly easily, so until the time is ripe to try the horse seriously we must exercise the greatest care.

They are, of course, still growing so their limbs, especially their joints, are very fragile. Keep to good, level ground and if it is in the least bit rough or uneven, walk. We do a lot of walking and very slow trotting on the road. The gentle concussion during road work not only hardens bone and tendons but also actually thickens the cortex of the bone. This greatly reduces the likelihood of sore shins later on when the horse is working on grass.

Shoeing is of paramount importance. 'No foot, no horse' is an adage to be remembered every day. It never ceases to amaze us how much damage can be done to the legs by feet being out of balance. Feet must be inspected every day to make sure that all horses are shod at the right time. A set of light training shoes only lasts the equivalent of about sixty miles of actual road work. And do not forget that unfit horses are more likely to drag their feet, especially hind feet, and may wear the toes out amazingly quickly. Incidentally, uneven wear of the hind shoes (i.e. one more than the other), is generally an indication of a back problem. *See* Appendix 1.

All of our horses go out in knee boots except when cantering on the all-weather track. These boots are attached below the knee so that if a horse does fall over he will, as it were, kneel on to the pad of the boot. Even in the most carefully controlled situation these young horses do stumble and fall occasionally. Our biggest dread, apart from jockeys being hurt, is a lacerated knee as the result of falling on the road. It almost always takes a long time to recover while the unfortunate owner goes on forking out for the keep. If such an accident befalls a two-year-old towards the end of the flat season it is a catastrophe for the owner who cannot know whether the horse is good enough to warrant keeping in training as a three-year-old. This is one way in which all-weather surfaces and all-year racing will be a godsend to owners.

If you should be unlucky enough to have such an accident happen, get the wound under a cold hose as quickly as possible and continue hosing for a good half hour. If the wound/laceration has penetrated below the skin, send for the vet and in the meantime a Jelonet dressing and wound powder should be applied. Any horse with an open wound of this kind must have a straw and not a shavings bed. To avoid such accidents as far as possible riders should always:

1. Keep out of range of other horses.
2. Ride with both hands on the reins.
3. Ride with the reins bridged.
4. Look where they are going.
5. Concentrate.

Nevertheless young horses do shy and lark about and do occasionally fall over.

Hind boots are worn if we find that a horse is in the least likely to knock himself behind. Overreach boots are also often needed, sometimes to stop a horse from pulling his front shoes off, which seems especially likely to happen with a misshapen front foot which has needed special attention from the farrier.

## A FIT HORSE

As the horse matures the work is gradually increased in both duration and intensity. Throughout this period the legs must be checked morning and evening to make sure that no undue strain is occurring. Symptoms will be heat, inflammation or soreness and are all warning signals that must not be disregarded. Never take a chance with these young animals because they are easily ruined. However, if all goes well, carry on. To start with, vary their work as much as you can, gradually increasing the number of canters a week. We like to take our horses out for a short ride first to get them settled down and then give them a canter on the all-weather track on the way home.

For older horses, like the eventers, we do quite a bit of interval training, but we have found this to be quite unsuitable for two-year-olds. They cannot do too much because they are so young, though they do take a couple of furlongs to settle down and get going, and if they are stopped as soon as they have started to go nicely they become unsettled and anxious. Interval training is too much for them both mentally and physically.

When cantering those that have been recently started, do not go too slowly. They actually find this more difficult. What they need is a nice swinging rhythm, with a jockey who is lightweight and out of the saddle.

By the time a horse is ready for serious work, he wants to be doing rides of four or five miles on non-cantering days and to be cantering three or four days a week with up to two steady canters of about six furlongs each. But, of course, all two-year-olds will reach this stage at different times. The backward ones who will not race until, say, September or October of their two-year-old year do not need to reach this stage until much later than those who are starting their racing career earlier in the season.

## A KEEN, ENTHUSIASTIC HORSE

Variety is the spice of life. When a horse does go into full training there is not nearly so much opportunity to vary the work or, indeed, the place of work. We try to work out as many different routes as possible and to vary the content of each ride as much as we can. With recently started ones, we like to take them into the woods and play follow-my-leader round the trees.

We try never to forget that a good racehorse must be competitive. It is important not to let any of them drop out of a canter and pull themselves up. If one does – and occasionally it happens, especially with a backward filly – put her up near the front of the string and try her upsides with a keen one, even a colt. Working upsides is something that always seems to inspire horses. They are, after all, bred to be competitive and going upsides is a sure way of brightening up a horse that lacks a bit of interest. Give her a change of jockey; this often works wonders. It is not necessarily the fault of the first lad, it is just one of those occasions when a change is as good as a tonic.

They love a canter in the stubble, on a woodland track or on a new headland (provided it has been harrowed and rolled) and they love to hack through the village or wherever there is something interesting to see.

We cannot emphasise too strongly that under no circumstances must a young horse be exhausted. Nothing kills their spirit as effectively as this.

## A BOLD HORSE

Continue the policy of making the horse you are starting take the lead. He was taught in the long reins to face the world on his own and he must be happy to go wherever the rider wants. Whenever possible, we make our horses take their own line. If, for example, we are

Fig 95 Yachtsman (Karen Dudley) and Ten No Trumps (Teresa Ellwood) giving a lead to pairs of two-year-olds upsides on the all-weather canter. Both riders in this picture are enjoying themselves and so are their horses.

Fig 96 Tara's Girl by Touching Wood, ex Esquire Lady (Samantha Mackintosh) and Face Up by Topville, ex Pomade (Daniel Minien).

115

Fig 97    Yabreen by Lypheor, ex Noble Mistress (Debbie Kay) and Trifolio by Touching Wood, ex Triple Reef (Marion Davey).

Fig 98    Tour Eiffel by High Line, ex Gay France (Kate Coldrey) and Sanctorum (Steve Mutton).

Fig 99 Simon Wilcock, a member of our 1988/89 team, riding Brave Question trained by Bill O'Gorman.

walking the string home from a ride out on the roads and we have to cross a field, we always make them spread out, abreast, and think for themselves. In this way we make sure that if we want to send a horse home early for any reason, he will willingly leave the others and not nap back to them.

Cantering upsides is very much a part of bravery training. Horses must learn to canter stirrup-to-stirrup so that they do not get rattled by the rough-and-tumble of a race. They soon learn to love it as it satisfies all their inbred competitiveness.

We are fortunate to have, mostly, very understanding drivers around Newmarket. It is of great importance that young horses do not get any nasty frights from inconsiderate road users. Once they realise that there is nothing to alarm them, and your old lead horse plays a big part here, they soon become safe in traffic.

With these four goals achieved our young racehorse is ready, physically and mentally, to get on with the serious job of winning races.

# 10

# Next Stages

## TURNING AWAY

Having started a young horse who is destined for a life other than racing, and got him going forward, straight and calmly as a two-year-old, we recommend turning him away for a year or so. There is no reason why he cannot be kept out all the time provided that you have a good field shelter, you keep the shelter bedded down with clean straw, you have a plentiful supply of clean water and you feed him plenty when the cold weather comes. And do not forget that he will still need his feet trimmed once a month and that he must be wormed monthly too. The more he is handled, the better, just to remind him that he was started and must not forget his manners.

Obviously, if the horse is a colt it is much better if he is gelded before being turned away. Indeed, in most circumstances it will be essential. Gelding is surprisingly untraumatic. However, to avoid pain and much swelling it is vital to keep on with exercise. We have ours gelded and allow complete recovery before turning away. Keep exercising as if nothing had happened and turn your gelding out in the afternoon as well. In this way he is unlikely to experience any ill effects. Geldings must be bedded on ultra-clean straw until the wound has completely healed. We spray the wound with Negasunt powder which keeps the flies off as well as healing.

Once the wound has healed and all swelling has gone (usually two or three weeks) you can turn him out full time, weather permitting. It is best to get this done by September to give him time to acclimatise to the onset of autumn and winter. Do not forget that it will be at least three months after gelding before a horse loses his libido, so do not turn him out with a mare or another colt until he has completely settled down.

Keep an eye on your young horse every day to make sure that all is well and that he is not losing condition. If he is you must step up the feeding. Equally if there is a lot of good grass be very very careful that there is not too much richness or your horse will end up with a case of laminitis. If there is any danger of this you must limit the intake of grass, either by bringing him in or by using a different 'starvation' paddock. In any case it is only by looking after him that you can be sure that he is getting the right amount of feed and is doing as he should. The old adage that the best muck is the farmer's footsteps applies equally to turned-out horses.

We prefer not to put rugs on our horses. Provided they can keep dry and have a nice deep bed in the field shelter they are better without. Of course, if they are not properly hardened off and have to go out in bad weather, then you must put on a really good, deep New Zealand rug. But unless it is well cut and a perfect fit it is better not to have one at all. A good New Zealand rug does not need a girth strap or surcingle, just leg straps behind. If it is a proper fit and a decent cut it will never move.

## RE-TRAINING AS A THREE-YEAR-OLD

If you decide to carry on with your horse as a three-year-old, get him up again early in the spring. He will be extremely soft so you must go very steady with him at first. Just to be on the safe side, we quickly go through the stages of starting again (lungeing, long reins, backing and riding away). He will need walking and very little trotting at first, gradually increasing until, probably in about a month, he is back where you left off when you turned him out.

This summer you can have a lovely time with him bringing him on quietly and steadily and teaching him, mostly without him knowing that he is being taught. One cannot generalise too much because horses mature at such different rates but a typical regime for a three-year-old might be:

**Monday**     Hack, about four to five miles walk and trot. Excellent if you have an older horse to encourage him. Let him be inquisitive and investigate odd things. Take him on lots of different going – grass, road, track, sand, wet, dry, etc. Do not forget that he is still young and his joints, tendons, etc. are easily damaged.

119

| | |
|---|---|
| **Tuesday** | Hack about two miles, then give him two steady canters of about six furlongs each (one in each direction if the canter is not straight). Then walk home for about one mile. |
| **Wednesday** | Hack about one to two miles, then do about twenty minutes maximum schooling in the manège. No small circles at canter. Forward movement must **never** be lost. If he starts to lose concentration, stop. |
| **Thursday** | As on Monday, preferably a different route. |
| **Friday** | As on Wednesday. When working in the school do not try and do too much. If you get your three-year-old going with a good rhythm at all paces and bending around your inside leg, all without losing forward movement, you will have done very well. |
| **Saturday** | Good long hack, preferably with a nice canter at some point. Leave him with good happy memories to consider over the weekend. |
| **Sunday** | Rest Day. Stand in or, in fine weather, turn him out for half a day (shorter if flies are a worry). It is a good idea to turn him out for a couple of hours every afternoon. |

Here are a few simple ways to improve your horse and make him more obedient.

**Forward movement**  This is the single most important factor. You will probably find that your horse will be sluggish going away from home and will want to hurry on the way back. Make him do the opposite, i.e. walk on going away and steady up coming back. Always walk out quietly and walk home for the last half-mile at the very least.

**Obedience**  Always avoid battles with the horse but by using your superior brain gradually let it become second nature for the horse to do what the rider asks. Much of your training can be done at the walk and you can have your way without any argument. Do not let your horse become used to doing the same thing at the same place every time. Where he thinks it is a good idea to canter, make him walk; if he expects to turn left, turn right; when you come to the gate on the way home, make him walk past it. In this and similar ways, you will soon have a horse that always does what the rider indicates and you will have won your battles without them taking place.

**Lateral work**   As we have just said, horses always want to hurry home. When you want to start doing a bit of leg yielding this is the ideal moment, because they will not lose their forward movement. The same applies later on to shoulder-in, half-pass, etc. Accompany the movement with the correct aids and, by the association of sensations, your horse will learn to respond to your aids with the movement you require.

**Obstacles**   Do not try to make your horse go through a small puddle that he can avoid. Wait until you have a good wide one right across the track and he will follow an older horse through it quite happily. When you find such a place, repeat the exercise several times, especially if he resisted at first, until he is walking through the water without any hesitation. If your horse shies at some strange object, do not hurry past, but let him approach it quietly (it may take a little time) and sniff at it, even touch it with his muzzle, until he is content that there is nothing to be scared of.

Teach him to stand still while you stop to admire the view, chat to a friend or investigate something in the hedge.

**Jumping**   There is no point in teaching your horse much about jumping as a three-year-old, unless he is going hurdling. In Britain, he is not allowed to jump at a show until he is four nor go to a horse trial until he is five. However, you can teach him to be brave by walking over fallen tree trunks or poles lying on the ground, or tiny streams and ditches. Always try to put him behind an older horse so that there is no fear or excitement as he negotiates his first obstacles.

# 11

# Conversion of Ex-Racehorses

There is much ill-informed prejudice against the Thoroughbred horse. The Thoroughbred is as varied as any other breed in temperament, ranging from extremely laid back to positively ferocious. Try giving a two-year-old cob 15lb of oats and having him out of his box for an hour a day and see what happens. However, a really difficult two-year-old colt often turns into a tractable three-year-old gelding and, as a four-year-old, can be a really outstanding riding or competition horse.

We love the Thoroughbred horse and consider him the best for many disciplines including racing, eventing and show-jumping. For courage and speed they are nonpareil and their jumping ability is beyond question. One thing, though, which distinguishes the Thoroughbred is sensitivity. They are quicker to react, easier to upset and take longer to forgive than more cold-blooded animals. For this reason they need more thought, more understanding and less forceful riding and handling than other breeds. But get it right and they will jump off the end of the world for you.

A similar prejudice exists against mares. A good mare is to a gelding what a Throughbred is to a Warmblood. They are loyal and trusting and will give you everything you ask and more once you have gained their complete confidence. Mares are like a certain little girl – When she was good she was very very good, but when she was bad she was horrid!

It is racing that exaggerates the difficult characteristics of the Thoroughbred. Those who have not been in training are no problem but one who has raced needs a period of sensible re-schooling to convert to a good competition horse. The question is always being asked about what happens to the hundreds of horses who go out of racing every year. We are spoilt for choice in Britain with such a wide variety of options to choose from. None the less there have always been, and always will be, lots of top horses in other fields who started their careers on the racecourse.

In many countries the ex-racehorse is the predominant competition horse for almost all other disciplines. For example, until very recently the US show-jumping team consistently beat the world on their lovely big Thoroughbreds, having evolved, under the brilliant leadership of Bert de Nemethy, a system of training perfectly suited to these horses. More recently, the Americans have gone for more warm-blooded types, not entirely to everyone's satisfaction and perhaps the Thoroughbred is already coming back into fashion. We hope so, for the US team gave us enormous pleasure on such glorious animals. The devotion of the North Americans to the pursuit of perfection has made them almost unbeatable, whatever they ride.

However, it is not only the United States. Australia, South Africa and New Zealand are all first-class equestrian nations who depend, to a great extent, on ex-racehorses for their stock of show-jumpers and eventers. Indeed, in Australia one of their Grand Prix dressage horses is called MCW, which stands for Melbourne Cup Winner. He is not, but at least he was bred for it and he certainly shows what a good conversion can do to transform a racehorse.

There are four stages in our system of conversion: rest and relaxation, re-schooling, reintroduction to the public and competition.

## REST AND RELAXATION

This is the stage between two completely different life-styles for the horse.

Instead of taking him straight out of racing it is a very good idea to let him right down and turn him away for a good long period so that all of the trauma and stress of his previous existence recede into the back of his mind. He will not forget, for horses have a prodigious memory, but turning out somehow seems to change a horse's attitude. All the tension can go (though it may come back later in some cases) and both mind and body can become relaxed. Visit the turned-out horse as much as possible, make a fuss of him, give him presents and handle him so that he enjoys contact with you. We recommend that such a horse is left turned out for several weeks until he is soft and relaxed.

# RE-SCHOOLING

We want everything to be as different as possible from the preparation for racing so that, as the horse gets fitter, it is part of a new way of life, not to be associated with the undoubted stress of training. We start off with at least a month in the loose school. This can be indoors or in an outside manège with high walls.

The first thing for our horse to learn is to go round the outside of the school. This can be done by using a guide rail about twelve feet (4m) from the outside wall. If this is difficult to organise it is better to have two people with lungeing whips standing on the centre line, guiding the horse around the outside of the school. The position of the body and the whip is exactly the same as for lungeing (*see* Chapter 3). You will need to get your horse word-perfect so that he will walk, trot, canter and change the rein on command.

If at first your horse gallops off around the school, let him do so. He will soon tire of it and, as he does, that is the moment to start taking charge and getting him to do as you want. You will find that very soon, and very easily, you will have him working perfectly to your voice. Never forget to praise him when he does well – be lavish with praise and affection and reward him with presents so that he glories in doing the right thing.

Do not be in too much of a hurry, for you are now laying the foundations for years of pleasure to come. When your horse is really settled, and you are satisfied that all is as you want, you can start him jumping. The first stage is to lay a pole on the ground on the long side of the school and let him sniff it, be led over it, walk over it and trot over it. Then add one or two more until he is calmly walking or trotting over poles without changing the rhythm of his stride. Do not let him turn away from a pole on the ground. If he does you have made a bad mistake.

There are two lessons that a horse must learn at this stage: the first is that jumping is easy and the second is that jumping is fun. Get these two ideas into his mind and you are half-way towards having a good jumper on your hands.

Now gradually introduce small fences like cavaletti into the school so that he is trotting and cantering calmly over them. Place them so that he has plenty of room to get at them and put good wings on the inside of the track to encourage him to jump. And so you work your way up until, about six weeks after you brought him in from his rest, he is jumping individual vertical and parallel fences up to 3ft 7in (1.10m), combinations of two fences and doing gymnastic exercises.

Either at the end of this period or a little earlier, if your horse is going calmly, you can start riding him again. Everything must be very relaxed at first, so that if you can go out for a quiet hack on a long rein, preferably with a trained horse to give you both confidence, you will be doing him a power of good. Gradually, you increase the amount of work you are doing until you are ready to institute a proper ridden training programme.

Once again it is forward movement that must be maintained but now you are introducing more advanced work. You must keep the forward movement going while teaching the horse to bend around your inside leg on the circle, staying on and accepting the bit. Introduce him to poles and fallen trees on the ground and gradually simulate the work you have done loose now that you are riding him.

Never get your young horse bored. If he does something really well, stop. Always finish your work on a good note and praise him and reward him so that he goes back to his stable happy and pleased with himself. Do not forget that he cannot take very long in the school – the concentration span is still short. We always try to work out a routine that is as varied as possible and teaches him as much as possible without him knowing that too many lessons have taken place. Your training programme could include:

1. Jumping.
2. Schooling in the manège (indoors and out).
3. Balance training – walking a horse over rough ground like ridge and furrow or steep hills with rocky outcrops on a loose rein is very good for this.
4. Bravery training – bursting through thickets, going through and along stream beds, crossing ditches, so that he becomes a go-anywhere, do-anything sort of horse.

Such a mixture of work each week will soon give you a bold, happy horse ready to give you a good ride whatever you want to do. Before long he will be ready to reappear in public.

# REINTRODUCTION TO THE PUBLIC
# AND COMPETITIONS

Be prepared for a little disappointment the first time your now perfectly-behaved horse goes to a public show of any kind. He may just associate it all with going racing and get very excited indeed. Ideally, you could take him off with another competition horse just to see the show without competing. If you can, ride him around for an hour or so until he is settled, then reward him and take him home again. The sooner he learns to stand around taking a calm and intelligent interest in what is going on, the better.

Try not to make his days too long, and above all do not overface or exhaust him. Let him find his early competitions fun and easy. He will soon know when he has done well and will take a real pride in it.

Now his conversion is well under way. If you are lucky enough to have found a horse with natural ability and if you have been patient, hard working, sympathetic and studious, you will now have that most desirable of all animals – a good young Thoroughbred on which to compete.

# 12

# Conclusion

Looking back over what we have written and studying Anthony Reynold's photographs, there seem to be a number of recurring themes which apply at every stage of horsemanship. Before making an analysis of these there is an important event that has been occupying the thoughts, conversation and writing of almost all horse people in Britain. This is the visit of the American horse-master, Monty Roberts, to Britain in 1989. We have adopted his word, starting, instead of breaking and anyone who saw him at work when he was here must acknowledge that he has a very special gift and technique with young horses.

However, when he started his exhibitions in Britain he was telling people that he was not specially gifted and that anyone who studied his methods could do the same. This is patently not the case and later in his tour people had to be warned not to try his method themselves unless they were sufficiently experienced. We do not believe that the accumulated knowledge of more than two thousand years, that has resulted in the system of starting young horses outlined in these pages, can be changed so dramatically by one man's ideas. The theory of 'advance and retreat' and the practice of 'linking up' are very nice expressions that Monty Roberts has formulated of fundamental truths about equines and we should be grateful for his very coherent and articulate description of them. But nothing can alter the fact that neither a young horse's mind nor his body are ready to accept a rider at the end of a total of 35 minutes' preparation. The system described in this book takes two to three weeks to arrive at the same stage (ridden loose in the lunge ring), and we guarantee that at the end of that period the horse who has been brought on steadily will be by far the better. He will more happily accept the bit, the rider's weight, the application of the rider's legs, the voice and will be more able to go forward and to go straight. We feel that we must add one special note of warning. Never, never put a roller/surcingle or a saddle on any horse, for the first time, without a breastplate. Without one, if the saddle slips back you have got yourself involved in a rodeo which will only end when something breaks and that something may be you.

Now, let us look for the recurring themes of the book.

## HAPPY HORSES

We talked about happy horses at the very beginning of this book. The message of people enjoying their work and of horses not only enjoying it but also finding it easy to accomplish, is reiterated all the way through. Horses have been put in the world for us to enjoy. If we make them happy they will do the same for us. They are for fun; if it is not fun to work with them, to ride them or to own them and watch them performing, then it is a waste of time and money.

## PRAISE AND REWARD

Like people, horses love to be praised when they have done well. Listen to anyone at any stage of the starting process and the thing you will hear most often, enunciated in the warmest of tones, is 'Good Boy/Girl'. Horses thrive on approval until, like the wonderful Desert Orchid, they achieve feats of unimaginable heroism to earn the praise of millions.

## FORWARD MOVEMENT

Forward movement is the most important factor at all stages of training any horse at any standard. It is the first lesson for any horse and, of course, is paramount in the case of a racehorse.

## TAKING TROUBLE

Slapdash methods never succeed. Those who achieve great success as trainers or riders are those who never rest in their pursuit of excellence. This becomes self-evident when you look at those who are at the top of their profession. Never take short cuts when working with horses for that is how accidents happen. Remember always to wear protective gear whenever advised to do so.

Fig 100 Christopher Coldrey and Nick Rogers (who is in charge of maintenance at Herringswell) discuss the going on the all-weather canter.

## PHYSICAL CONDITION

No athlete, least of all a horse, can give of his best unless he feels marvellous. If your horse is not performing well, look first for a physical problem which, when put right, will solve your problems.

## ASKING TOO MUCH

Never ask too much of a young horse, especially in the early stages of starting. They simply cannot take it physically or mentally. If they go well and then start to resist, it is a sure sign that you have gone on too long. Do not forget that their attention span is very short. Remember that the limbs of yearlings and two-year-olds are 'made of glass', so be careful to work them on very level ground and if you come to a bad place, walk through it.

## VARIETY

Try and vary the work and the place that you do it as much as possible. This keeps a horse interested in what he is doing and puts

Fig 101 New intake. First yearlings to arrive for starting from the USA in August 1989. Left to right: ch. colt Diesis, ex Informative trained by Henry Cecil; b. colt Verbatim, ex Agujita trained by Henry Cecil; gr. colt Danzig, ex Sintra trained by Michael Stoute; b. colt Secreto, ex Overstate trained by Michael Stoute. They are owned by Sir Gordon White.

Fig 102 Top Lot from Goffs sales in Ireland, a lovely bay colt by Sadlers Wells, ex Forlene, looking calm and relaxed on arrival at Herringswell. Trained by Michael Stoute.

more 'miles under his belt', giving him more experience of the world and making him calmer and braver.

## BE FIRM

Do not be tentative in your approach. Always let a horse know you are there, that you are affectionate but firm, that you are ready to praise, but will not be put upon. Handle the horse firmly but gently. When grooming or patting for praise do not dab at the horse but let him feel your firmness and confidence. This gives the horse confidence in himself and in you.

So there it is. This extraordinary animal consumes our time, energy and money to a degree that often seems totally disproportionate to any benefits that might accrue. But man's obsession with this noble creature has endured for millennia and will endure for millennia yet to come. The fact is that whatever hardships he inflicts on us, we, *Homo sapiens,* have discovered in the horse a puzzle and a challenge which amply repays a lifetime of study.

# Appendix 1

## EQUITHERAPY – PHYSIOTHERAPY FOR HORSES

It is not so long ago that doctors regarded chiropractors and osteopaths as dangerous quacks and would hear nothing in their favour. Along with acupuncture and homoeopathy, their work was viewed as a fraudulent challenge to proven and conventional medicine. Today, many qualified doctors practise these techniques themselves, others call practitioners in to help in appropriate cases and even use their services to relieve their own aches and pains.

Unfortunately there is still much scepticism and even downright disapproval among some veterinarians concerning the work of the equitherapists. This is not at all surprising because the claims made by some of them have been manifestly impossible. The vets say that assertions concerning the manipulation of the horse's spine cannot, physically, be true and as a result they have disregarded the work that the 'back people' have been doing. However, there can be no doubt that, whatever they said and thought they were doing, they were in fact doing good. Many a horse who would otherwise have been finished, as well as suffering a lot of pain, has been restored to full health and vigour by treatment from the equine physiotherapists.

Just as doctors must listen to their patients (because the key to diagnosis may lie in what they say), so veterinarians must listen to the horse keepers. Those of us dealing with hundreds of horses all the time will surely know best whether a treatment has worked or not. We are sure that all who keep horses on any scale and who have experience of the work of a good equitherapist will agree that they constantly achieve remarkable and lasting cures.

Fortunately there are now a number of highly qualified physiotherapists who are working with horses. They can speak to vets in authoritative terms which give them common ground. It is truly essential, in the interests of the horse, that they are brought into the fold as a recognised adjunct to the veterinary profession. It is highly undesirable when horsekeepers themselves have to call in the therapist and hope their vet will not call in and find them at work. It is the vet who should be calling in the therapist to help with a problem he has diagnosed. Of course, like all new ideas, foolish people build up the case for equitherapy with stupid claims and have expectations which cannot be realised. It is not snake oil – a cure-all that will solve every problem – it is simply a branch of veterinary medicine which can achieve absolutely splendid results in a great many cases.

People often ask if back therapy lasts or do the horses get recurring back problems. The answer is, that just as with people, some backs are stronger than others. One horse could have an accident, receive treatment, and never suffer again, another might go several months after successful therapy and then because of some innate weakness, need further treatment from time to time.

## Back Problems and their Relief in Horses

We all know how debilitating it is when we have a bad head, neck or back ache. Active people, such as athletes, cannot possibly work properly if they are suffering in this way. But they at least can tell us what is hurting and what other symptoms they have, so helping us to help them. The poor old horse cannot do this, so there is a real responsibility on the part of riders and trainers to notice any symptoms that indicate that their horse has a problem.

Here, we will try to explain what you should look for so that you can call in the equitherapist to help. Under no circumstances should you attempt any of this work yourself. If you have a problem you should consult your vet, and if it is a situation where the particular skills of an equitherapist are required, it is to be hoped that your vet will call one in to treat your horse. Over the next few pages we shall consider the likely causes of back problems and what symptoms to look for. As you read, think of your own back and how what is said here equates with your own personal experience.

**Slipping and sliding** If a horse slips and one leg shoots out, especially on a slippery road, you can see how it will jar the back.
**Shying** As above. If a horse suddenly jumps away from a disturbance the same can happen.

**Getting cast**  I expect most people who keep horses have seen one cast in his box. This is when a horse lies down too close to the wall, cannot get his legs out to get up and cannot roll over to get more room. If you see this happening and the poor horse struggling to get up and thrashing about on the ground, it will not surprise you if his back is wrenched and injured.

**Pulling back**  If something frightens a horse who is tied up, he will sometimes pull back and hurt himself. In this case the axis-joint is likely to be very slightly displaced. Never tie a horse up except with a string which will break in an emergency. Otherwise they can lose their footing and hang themselves.

**Lungeing**  If a lunger is too strong with his hands and yanks the horse's head inwards the same axis-joint displacement can occur.

**Jumping off**  A sudden burst of energy from standing to gallop in very few strides can sometimes strain a horse's back.

**Landing**  This is an obvious cause of potential back problems. Course designers should try and not include too many steep drops in their cross-country courses.

**Falling**  Like all athletes and sports players, horses will inevitably fall from time to time. When they do, it is probable that they will injure their back, at any point from head to tail.

## Symptoms

Whenever any of the above occur, be on the look-out for any of these symptoms:

**The horse crouches when you get on**  You do get the odd horse who always flinches when mounted. But generally a therapist should be called in if the horse does not like either being saddled or mounted. The old idea that many horses had 'cold backs' is one which can nearly always be put right with treatment.

**The horse is not the same when trotting on both diagonals**  Initially, almost all young horses find it easier for the rider to rise to the trot on one diagonal than the other. But if this difference is very great, or if it becomes more pronounced it should be rectified. This can nearly always be done with little problem.

**Cantering**  If your horse is unwilling to canter on one rein it may be symptomatic of a back problem which needs attention. The same applies in the case of a horse who canters disunited. All this bears out what we said earlier about most problems being physical ones. They cannot be schooled out but need attending to by a vet or therapist.

**The horse finds turning difficult**   You may find that your horse turns or circles more easily to the left than to the right. At the beginning of a horse's training this is normal, but if it is exaggerated or becomes worse, treatment is indicated and will be effective.

**Uneven wear of the shoe behind**   Weak and unfit horses tend to drag their toes anyway, but if you find a horse is going through his hind shoes unduly fast, or if he is wearing out one shoe much faster than the other, it is a good indication of back trouble.

**Flinching at the withers**   A lot of horses are a bit sensitive to touch around the withers, but if you find that a horse is really flinching to the touch either on or below the withers, you can bet he needs treatment. You can tell quite easily whether he is being sensitive or whether he is in pain.

**Bad temper**   A horse in pain is likely to be irritable, so do not write him off as an ill-natured beast. Check thoroughly to see if there is a reason for his bad temper which can perhaps be put right.

**Bucking or rearing**   Both these vices can be symptoms of back ache. Check this first before you take more drastic measures.

## Treatment

There are basically four areas of the back that can be treated. They are:

1. The axis joint.
2. The withers and ribs.
3. The lumbar region of the spine.
4. The sacro-iliac joint.

We are certainly not qualified to discuss the technicalities or methods of treatment, but it seems to us that it is two-fold. First, there are some areas which can be manipulated and others which cannot. The therapist manipulates some joints, where necessary using the horse's own weight to help in the process. The second treatment consists of releasing and easing muscles which are in spasm which results in greatly helping to remove pain.

There are many machines on the market which enhance the curing process in equine injuries. They need expert use and no one should buy or use one except on the advice and instruction of a vet or qualified therapist.

# Appendix 2

## THE FOOT

'No foot, no horse.' The truest thing ever said! Here is Xenophon again, on the subject of buying a horse. Predictably, for he was a marvellous horseman, the first thing he looks at are the feet.

> To begin with, I shall describe how a man, in buying a horse, would be least likely to be cheated. In the case of an unbroken colt, of course his frame is what you must test; as for spirit, no very sure signs of that are offered by an animal that has never yet been mounted. And in his frame, the first things which I say you ought to look at are his feet. Just as a house would be good for nothing if it were very handsome above but lacked the proper foundations, so too a war-horse, even if all his other points were fine, would yet be good for nothing if he had bad feet; for he could not use a single one of his fine points.
>
> The feet should first be tested by examining the horn; thick horn is a much better mark of good feet than thin. Again, one should not fail to note whether the hoofs at toe and heel come up high or lie low. High ones keep what is called the frog well off the ground, while horses with low hoofs walk with the hardest and softest part of the foot at once, like knock-kneed men. Simon says that their sound is a proof of good feet, and he is right, for a hollow hoof resounds like a cymbal as it strikes the ground.

People often talk of a foot being in or out of balance. As this is of special importance in young horses, Darren Rose has kindly written the following piece for us. He makes reference to John Hickman and Dr Doug Butler.

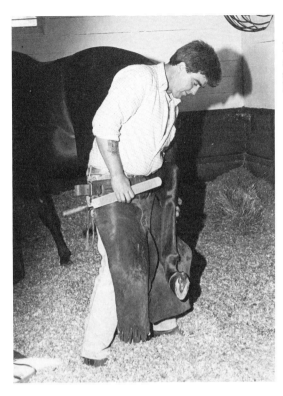

Fig 103  Mark Rose, AWCF checking the symmetry of a yearling's hind foot.

## Hoof Balance

Hoof balance is the assessment of the ground-bearing surface of the hoof capsule in relation to the long axis of the limb. This is attained by removing the shoe and cleaning the foot, holding the limb just below the carpus and keeping it in line with the horse's natural flight pattern. With the horse's limb relaxed, the hoof capsule will hang freely (unrestricted). Look along the long axis and in the area of the buttresses of the heels imagine a line at 90 degrees to the long axis. The hoof capsule's ground-bearing surface should be prepared in relation to this imaginary line.

Once the ground-bearing surface is balanced, the limb should be taken forward in front of the horse and hung over one's own knee, looking down the limb to note any flares of horn or deviation of limb. Any flares of horn should be removed to create a symmetrical shape to the horny capsule. Once achieved, the horse must be stood square on level ground and an assessment made looking for symmetry.

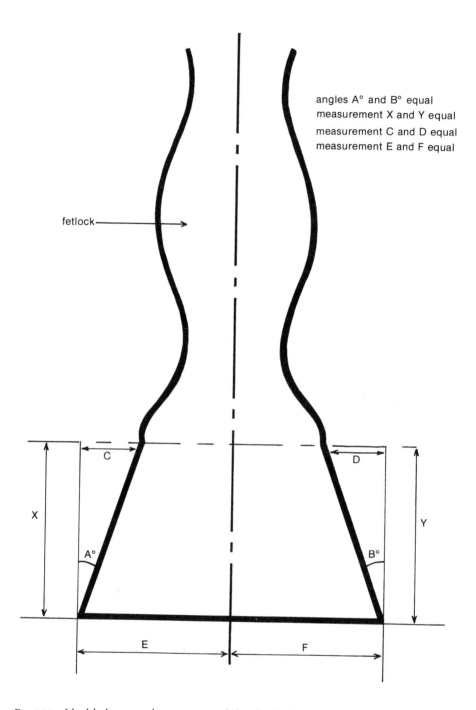

angles A° and B° equal
measurement X and Y equal
measurement C and D equal
measurement E and F equal

fetlock

C

D

X

Y

A°

B°

E

F

Fig 104  Ideal balance and symmetry of the forelimb.

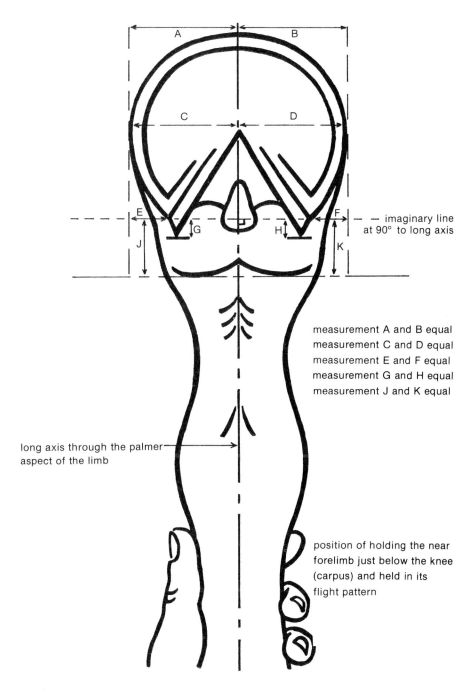

imaginary line
at 90° to long axis

measurement A and B equal
measurement C and D equal
measurement E and F equal
measurement G and H equal
measurement J and K equal

long axis through the palmer
aspect of the limb

position of holding the near
forelimb just below the knee
(carpus) and held in its
flight pattern

Fig 105   Bi-lateral symmetry, anterior view.

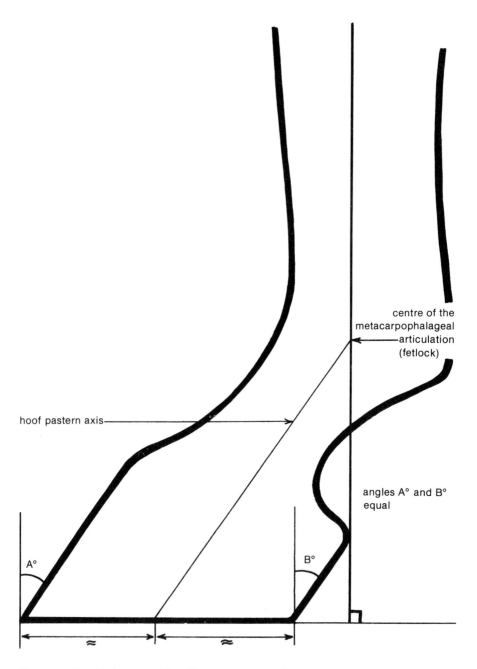

centre of the
metacarpophalageal
—articulation
(fetlock)

hoof pastern axis————

angles A° and B°
equal

A°

B°

Fig 106  Hoof balance and hoof/pastern axis in the
ideal forelimb.

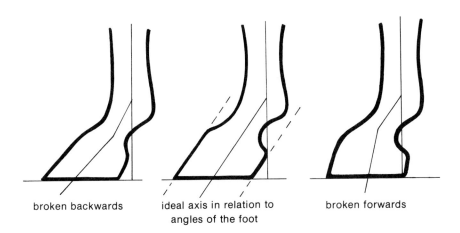

broken backwards    ideal axis in relation to    broken forwards
angles of the foot

Fig 107   Angles and axes.

**Note**  Most young stock turn their toes in. This can be due to the fact that the animal is narrow chested and when full in the chest the toes will turn out to a natural conformation (assuming that the feet are balanced). Also, an assessment is made of the limb from the lateral aspect of the horse, assessing a natural hoof/pastern axis (HPA), a broken-forward HPA or a broken-back HPA. Any deviation from the correct conformation should be corrected.

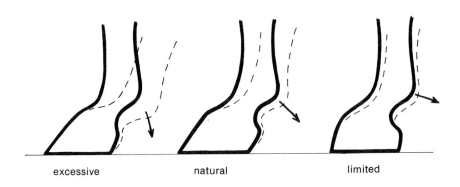

excessive    natural    limited

Fig 108   Rotation in relation to axes.

## Hoof/Pastern Axis

Hoof/pastern axis is most important when assessing the conformation of a horse as any abnormalities can create problems, i.e. a broken-forward HPA creates excessive pressure on the metacarpo phalangeal articulation (fetlock) and on the palmer aspect of the foot. This can also be termed as the 'long toe, low heel' syndrome, being detrimental in the long term, affecting the joints of the digit and placing the tendons under excessive strain. In the case of a broken back HPA, limited pressure would create concussion because of the upright confirmation.

**Note** The function of the fetlock is to act as the horse's shock absorption system as each stride is taken and under the influence of body-weight the joint rotates and causes rotation in the lower articulations. This hinge-like movement 'dampens' the concussive forces but can only operate correctly if the axis is normal.

# Index

age, 26

backing, 80
Ballantyne, Stephen, 73
Birchall, Melanie, 80
body, position of, 38, 39, 41, 42, 49, 124
boots, 33, 40, 60, 112, 113
Bunker, Mari-Lynn, 44

Cecil, Henry, 11, 20, 34, 44, 80, 130
Coldrey, Charles, 46, 50, 51, 84
Coldrey, Kate, 116
commands, 42, 43
concentration, 43, 63, 113, 120, 125

Davey, Marion, 34, 116
De Nemethy, Bert, 123
diagonal, correct, 97
dressage, 11, 12, 26
Dudley, Karen, 51, 86, 88, 115

electrolytes, 29
Ellwood, Teresa, 86, 88, 115
equitherapy, see physiotherapy

feeding, 103, 118
feet, 21, 33, 60, 105, 112, 118, 135, 136-43
forward, 64, 88, 92, 95, 96, 97, 98, 120, 125, 127, 128

gelding, 118

Hall, Anita, 84, 85
Hernon, John, 73
Herringswell Bloodstock Centre, 6, 9, 18, 78, 111, 129, 130
hoof balance, 137
hoof/pastern axis, 143

interval training, 113

jumping, 121, 125

Kaye, Debbie, 23, 68, 116

lateral work, 121
lead horse, 89, 95, 97, 98, 117
lunge ring, 31, 32, 40, 81, 82

Mackintosh, Samantha, 115
Minien, Daniel, 115
minimum requirements, 20
Mutton, Steve, 116

Nash, Niamh, 93

obedience, 120
obstacles, 121
O'Gorman, Bill, 40, 56, 93, 117

Phrogg, Sep, 56
physiotherapy, 37, 106, 109, 132-5
praise, 34, 42, 54, 79, 81, 124, 125, 128, 131
Prescott, Sir Mark, 7, 51, 68, 73

rein, change of, 65, 66, 67
  holding the, 36
reschooling, 124-5
Reynolds, Anthony, 6, 51, 127
riding away, 82
Roberts, Monty, 7, 11, 12, 85, 127
Rogers, Nick, 129
Rose, Daren, 6, 105, 136
Rose, Mark, 6, 22, 105, 137
rugs, 45, 69, 70, 119
rhythm, 40, 54, 113, 120

Seager, Sharon, 57
shoes, *see* feet
side reins, 55, 56, 57, 62, 63, 69,
  75
Spanish Riding School, 71
Stoute, Michael, 130

tacking up, 32, 67
teeth, 31, 104
  wolf, 104-5
titbits, 35
turning away, 118

variety, 129
Vickerman, Emily, 72

Walton, Stuart, 81, 83, 86, 90
Whitwood, Carol, 6, 106, 107-8
Wilcock, Simon, 117
worms, worming, 103, 118
Wragg, Geoff, 57

Xenophon, 12, 17-18, 98-9, 136

M .